Your friend.
Ballard S. Dunn.

BRAZIL,

THE

HOME FOR SOUTHERNERS:

OR,

A PRACTICAL ACCOUNT OF WHAT THE AUTHOR,
AND OTHERS,
WHO VISITED THAT COUNTRY, FOR THE SAME OBJECTS,
SAW AND DID WHILE IN THAT EMPIRE.

BY

REV. BALLARD S. DUNN,

RECTOR OF ST. PHILLIP'S CHURCH, NEW ORLEANS,
AND LATE OF THE CONFEDERATE ARMY.

NEW YORK:
GEORGE B. RICHARDSON,
540 BROADWAY.

BLOOMFIELD & STEEL,
NEW ORLEANS.
1866.

PREFACE.

THIS little book lays no claim to literary merit. It is a plain, true story, for honest, true people. It is written for such Southerners as are seriously contemplating expatriation, from manly motives. No attempt has been made, at giving *reasons*, why any should leave this country. If those into whose hands it may fall, have not already good, and sufficient reasons, for quitting the United States, I should be the last to furnish anything of that nature. On the contrary, if any simply propose to themselves to seek a country where they can accumulate more rapidly, the first advice I should venture, would be, that they should remain where they are. Not that I believe they could not improve their pecuniary condition by emigrating to Brazil, but because this is an unworthy motive from which to leave one's country.

And, to be right candid with such, we do

not desire them. If they have no higher, nobler, more painful motive than this, and only flee now from the federal tax-gatherer; it would not be difficult to trace them back, and identify them with that class who failed in their duty; who shrunk from sacrifices, when sacrificing might have availed. Such men are not good members of society, and therefore not desirable in the community we hope to establish.

Nor is this a book that has anything to say about the *constitootional* amendment: it cannot then reasonably be expected that it will suddenly become *very* popular *literatoor*, among the politico-religionists of the North, any more than with the professional politicians of the South.

All of this, too, from the same cause. For these two glorious fraternities have at last met on the same platform. And what seems singular, is the fact, that a platform which is expected to bear up so many, and those, too, upon whose shoulders rest the future glory and vastness of the republic, should have but one plank: and that the doubtful one, of the meekness, long suffering, pusillanimous cowardice, and great facility in belying their entire history, on the part of the South; while they make the welkin ring with hosannas for the conquering North; and evince the greatest degree of obsequious readiness to do anything they are bid, by the all-powerful, all-glorious, ALL-WISE, UNAPPEASABLE.

This platform is adopted by the politico-religionists, alias, radicals; because it is agreeable to their feelings, and in accordance with their sentiments and antecedents: they, being the "Saints of the Lord," have a right to triumph over their fallen enemies. It is adopted by Southern politicians, because they believe that nothing short of the absolute degradation and infamy of the Southern people, voluntarily taken upon themselves, can ever give them office again, and companionship with those they woo so affectionately.

I have met many Southern office seekers, since my return, and I hope I may be pardoned, if I attempt to invent a comparison, that will illustrate, somewhat, my idea of their physical appearance, and moral condition. If you can conceive of a gang of old hyenas, that have been kept for four years in cages, upon half rations of green persimmons, and poked up, daily, by a lot of mischievous boys, with sharp sticks (no allusion to bayonets), suddenly calming down; and then attempting, with great earnestness, to look sweet, and amiable, and dove-like; and even evincing a disposition to caress the dear boys (radicals) that poked them, you have an illustration of what has happened. But the carniverous instincts of the animal will appear. They may point to the persimmon stain, as evidence that they are not men eaters, but it is no go. *The hyena will out.* Consequently, the dear boys decline the caresses.

NEW YORK, Oct. 6, 1866.

BRAZIL.

CHAPTER I.

OUR PRESENT CONDITION IN THE SOUTH.

When the morning light begins to dawn, after a long night of sorrowing anxiety and watching, its first beams are grateful to our eyes, even though they find us heart-riven mourners, weeping over all that remains of a loved one gone before. And, as time flows onward, and the rolling seasons bring again bright, beautiful Easter, with its vernal flowers, sweet emblems of the resurrection, we learn how to heed the voice of inspiration, and "mourn, not as those without hope." But alas! not so with our political condition in the South! The gloomy night of sorrow, and of death, has been lengthened out to four long and bloody years. The weary watchers who have fallen asleep, to wake no more, this side the judgment day, are numbered by hundreds of thousands.

The lurid morning that struggles, and alternates between darkness and dawning, bewildering, and disheartening indeed, can, at best, promise a day little better than the night.

When this is so patent, to all who view our present condition in the broad light of history, shall any Southerner be blamed, if he seeks a land where the night of vengeance has not come, that his day may not be one of threatening? Why should he? For, as surely as that these four years of disastrous war have left most of those who have been true to themselves and their ancestors penniless, homeless, despoiled, and bereaved, so surely the future, with its cumbrous disabilities, and fearful forebodings, promises nothing better than poverty and humiliation: with no guarantee that worse, even, than these may not befall. The late scenes at Memphis and New Orleans, with many others, of like character, throughout the South, not permitted to find their way into the public prints, are but the precursors of those awful anarchical struggles that precede all radical changes in governments that have grown suddenly great, powerful, and unscrupulous: whose greatness and power, because wicked and corrupt, end in self-destruction. Those who oppress you, are energetic, aggressive, ambitious, and ravenous. In them you see foulness of life, and cruelty of policy, methodized into a system; consecrated by their religion; and these must be gratified; peacefully, and unresisted if possible, violently, and with the sword, if necessary. The power that now holds you, like so many captives, bound to the stake, while it decides, as barbarians have done before, whether it is better to burn, flay alive, or release; while we see in it none of the elements of permanency, or stability, is appalling enough; in the hands of such as are sufficiently vigorous and unscrupulous to set it in motion. Then why should we remain in a country, where we find that there is neither present, nor prospective, security, for life, liberty and property? Where we are painfully conscious of the fact, that our chiefest privilege is, to pay exorbitant taxes, to meet the demands of the debt incurred in our subjugation; and to pay the enhanced salaries of those who have grown glorious by butchering our kindred, destroying our cities and towns, our fields and firesides; and insulting our women, as they robbed, and turned them, and our little ones, out into the storm and night? Some counsel us to stand our ground; to stick to the soil that gave us birth, and *root* them out.

If the little mouse, with her helpless family plowed up in midwinter, with all her darlings cut in twain, by the cruel ploughshare; and one of her own limbs severed from her benumbed, and enfeebled body, should say to herself, "I'll stand my ground, and to-morrow, when he comes to plough again, I'll bite his horse's hoofs, and drive him away;" it would be about as sensible, and about as hopeful of results, as this rooting policy which many propose. It sounds very absurd, after having laid down our arms, and taken a solemn parole to use them no more, only to find no abatement of the malignity of those who style the victors conquerors, for sane persons to talk about *rooting* them out. As well might you expect the feeble Texas cow-boy, who stalks vacantly after his ureasoning herd, would put forth his irresolute arm, bind the icy pinions of the furious north wind, that blights his native plains, remanding him back to the snowy cliffs from whence he came, with a "peace be still;" as to imagine that your time-serving resolutions, proclaimed at cross-road political meetings, or your coalescent conventions, inaugurated for the purpose of training and managing politicians, in whom you, yourselves, have no confidence, whom the world justly despises, will stay the rapacity, or mitigate the cruelty, of those who wrought your ruin.

No, indeed! I have no confidence in the swinish drill, as a means of restoration and redemption. You may pass resolutions until you exhaust the prolific fountain of political falsehood and deception; and root, till you wear you noses off, and then find yourselves about as happy, and successful, as the individual who severed the same member to "spite his face."

The rooting army, who are just beginning to discover how valiantly patriotic they are, invariably inform you, after announcing their tactics, that there is a great deal of good feeling growing up between the Northern people, and the Southern people. To prove that such is the fact, they will tell you that they heard such and such a Northern general speak, in terms of admiration, of Stonewall Jackson, and of General Lee's military genius. This indicates the *mode* in which they would be pleased to carry on this undermining warfare.

The first grand consideration is, to have it as free from danger as may be; for the rank and file, of this noble army, are generally such as kept out of harm's way; therefore, they are pleased to see these tokens of friendship, passing, and repassing.

Gallant, but peaceful scavenger-warriors, you must excuse me; for I tell you frankly, that I have as little confidence in the sincerity of these hollow compliments, as I have in your proposed mode of getting back our lost rights.

When I travel through the North, where we are apt to hear such compliments, in the offering of which, the mental reservation contains the very life principle, and guiding star of those who thus attempt to deceive for a purpose, which purpose is private gain; and am entertained, by paying for more than I receive, upon substance taken, very likely, by violence, from my native State, by those who enjoy the felicity of having discovered that theft is no crime; murder not reprehensible; and that which is worse than murder, the peculiar prerogative of the patriotic: hear, perhaps, the familiar tones of the identical piano, over whose keys once swept, with magic power, the taper fingers of my own loved cousins, tortured by the clumsy paws of one who never could have been mistress of such an instrument, but for the fortunes of war; see, possibly, upon the shelves of a Massachusetts cobbler, the choice volumes of a Southern gentleman's library; or hear the harsh voice of a New England auctioneer, crying off, to the highest bidder, the rare paintings of the first masters, the accumulations of years of judiciously exercised taste, (stolen from the same Southern homes, from whence came the silver plate, which, though shipped by tyrants high in rank, it was deemed expedient that it should go as "soiled linen;") I am forcibly reminded of the fable of the lion, who was entertained by the man. Mr. Lion had the run of the palace, in which there were many things to be admired. There were large saloons, and long corriders, richly furnished and decorated, and filled with a profusion of fine specimens of sculpture and paintings, the works of the finest artists. The subjects represented were various, but the most prominent of them all, had an especial interest for the noble animal that stalked by them. It was that of the lion himself; and as the owner of the mansion led him from one apartment into another, he did not fail to direct his attention to the indirect homage these various groups and tableaux, paid to the importance of the lion tribe. There was, however, one remarkable feature in all of them, upon which the host was silent; which was, that diverse as were these representations, there was one point in which they all agreed. It was this. The man was always victorious, the lion always overcome. The man had it all his own way, and the lion was but a fool, to make him sport. There were exquisite works in marble, of Samson rending the lion like a kid; and young David taking the lion by the beard and choking him.

There was the man who ran his arm down the

lion's throat, and held him fast by the tongue; and there was that other, who, when carried off in his teeth, contrived to pull a knife from his pocket, and lodge it in the heart of the monster. Then there was a lion hunt, or what had been such; for the brute was rolling round in the agonies of death, and his conqueror, on his bleeding horse, was surveying him at a safe distance.

There was a gladiator from a Roman amphitheatre, in mortal struggle with his powerful foe, but it was plain who was getting the mastery. There was a lion in a net, and a lion in a trap; four lions, yoked in harness, were drawing the car of a Roman Emperor: and elsewhere stood Hercules, clad in the lion's skin. Nor was this all. The lion was not only triumphed over, mocked, and derided; but he was tortured into extravagant forms, as if he were not only the creature and menial of man, but the work of man's creation. He became an artist's decoration, and an heraldic emblazonment. The feet of alabaster tables fell away into lions' paws; lions' faces grinned on each side the shining mantle piece; and lions' mouths held tight the handles of the doors. There were sphinxes, too, half lion and half woman; there were lions rampant, holding flags; lions couchant, lions passant, lions regardant; lions and unicorns; there were lions white, lions black, and lions red. In short, there was no variety of misconception and indignity which was thought too great to put upon the lord of the forest, and the king of beasts. After he had gone over the mansion, his entertainer asked him what he thought of the splendors it contained: and the lion, in return, did full justice to the riches of its owner, and the skill of its decorators, but he added; "Lions had fared better, had lions been the artists." The application is obvious.

The Southerner who reads the accounts of the great battles that have been fought, which are now passing into permanent history, and has access to a file of Northern pictorials; finds himself depicted as a powerful, dangerous, warlike beast of prey; but always vanquished; always overcome; always humbled; and then caricatured, by the born citizens of the Union: most of whom, however, when they came in contact with us on the field of battle, or fell into our hands as prisoners of war, managed to speak a foreign language. To me, the deceitful, hypocritical, cunning devices, employed by the cowardly, grasping puritan, to enable him to reap, without danger, the fruits of a victory won by others, are worse than mockery. And when they urge me to forget the past, that we may all be brethern together, my sense of justice teaches me that there should be a corresponding relaxation, in good faith, on their part. I feel that I ought at least, to be permitted to mark the resting-place of my poor dead brother, or my Bishop, with a monument that, while it sings not of victory, nor defeat, would be in some measure, a testimonial of my appreciation of his merits as a man, and a Christian.

No, indeed! when I am asked to forget the thousand instances in which the strong arm upon which the weak leaned, the warm heart in which they confided, and the clear head to which they trusted to carry them through, are now stilled in death; and to credit fiction, that I know to be basely false, and an insult to High Heaven, my answer is, no, never. For though they be dead, and buried, without winding sheet, other than their tattered uniforms; without requiem, other than the fierce rattle of musketry, the roar of artillery, and the fearful crash of bursting shells, they shall not be forgotten.. Though they moulder now, in yonder shapeless mounds of blood-stained earth, the unsung heroes of a fruitless struggle; sadly misrepresented on the distorted page of history; yet shall they live in our hearts, till life and memory perish. And then, when we are about to follow them, we will charge our little ones to continue to honor and revere the memory of the heroic dead. And we will continue to pray for those noble leaders, who languish still in prison, uncondemned, or falsely condemned; asking the great and good God, to "give them a happy issue out of all their afflictions."

CHAPTER II.

CONFLICTING STATEMENTS CONSIDERED.

It will be very natural for home-folks to ask, "How are we to harmonize the accounts of those who return from Brazil, abusing the country, and the inhabitants; and confidently asserting, that it is not suitable, nor desirable for Southerners; with the enthusiastic descriptions of those who return for their friends, and are actively preparing to adopt that country as their home?"

The best answer to this question, and the one most likely to do all parties justice, will be to relate once more, the fable of the two Knights, who fought, each for the truth of what he saw with his own eyes, and because his report was contradicted by the other. They met at a monument, one on either side. The first speaker was extravagant in his praise of the gold work on the shield of the warrior engraven upon the monument. The second was equally enthusiastic in his admiration, but asserted that it was silver. Upon this issue they fought, furiously, until both were severely wounded, and unhorsed: when each, falling upon the ground occupied by his antagonist when the contest began, looked up, and saw that the shield was gold on one side, and silver on the other. So that both had been right, and both wrong. But unlike the report of the Knights in this fable, the data upon which these conflicting statements are made are not equally good, nor equally coextensive with the subject in dispute.

Let us examine, first, the travelling record of the bearer of bad news. He shall be Sir Knight of the golden side. This individual has made the most of the privileges generally accorded to such messengers in well regulated society; in that he speaks first, keeps on speaking, and is encouraged to continue, by his applauding hearers, who are generally such as "knew the horse would eat up the grind-stone."

Sir Knight of the golden side, being a gentleman of elegant leisure, and in no danger of prosecution, as he had never raised a finger against the "best government," took care to wait long enough, after the "break up" in the South, to find the railroads leading to New York repaired, and a comfortable line of steamers established between that city and Rio de Janiero, upon one of which he embarked, vowing and declaring that the land of the Southern Cross, and of tropical fruits, should be his home for the future. On board this steamer, he is sure to find some one who is willing to give him information as to whom he had better apply for further information, on reaching Brazil. Accordingly, he takes his new friend's advice; and on reaching the Brazilian capital, goes straight to Mr. Shylock, deposits his gold, gets some small currency for convenience, and then, Mr. Shylock, who combines in himself many avocations, being real estate broker, house-to-let agent, boarding house runner, with various other profitable employments, soon fits him out with a house, if he has his family along, and wishes to keep house; or directs him to a proper place to board. At every turn, the desired information pours in upon him, and additional parties are indicated, who are capable of giving more. So that the new comer soon finds himself surrounded by the warmest kind of friends; who all concur in deprecating the unfortunate move that brought him and his interesting family, for a mere political pique, from a country so great and prosperous as the United States, to one so insignificant and treacherous as Brazil. They will even startle his astonished and indignant imagination by roundly asserting, that there is not a man in the Empire they cannot buy: that everything goes by favoritism, bribery, fraud, and rascality: and as for the government keeping faith with anybody, that is simply absurd.

They continue their discourse something like the following: "Besides, you Southerners are an agricultural people: you do not wish to settle in any country where the land is so wretchedly poor as you see these barren hills are; and so steep, too, that a goat can scarcely keep his footing. What you see, is a sample of the whole." Then they conclude by advising Sir Knight of the golden side to take a run out on the Dom Pedro Segunda Railroad, that he may see for himself, that all they have told him is verity and truth. Overwhelmed with their disinterested friendship, and thoroughly convinced of their wisdom, and the matchless manner in which they state the whole case, he can do no less than take their advice to the letter. So off he goes, with the view of verifying what he already religiously believes. Full twelve hours have elapsed, when he returns, filled with indignation against Brazil, and the Brazilians. The land is as poor as poverty, for he has seen it with his own eyes. The people are depraved, and debauched in morals, as well as diseased and decrepid in body. Henceforward, until he is ready to return to the United States, he walks the streets of Rio de Janiero, with head erect, chest thrown forward, shoulders backward, toes outward; with a movement of his magnificent person so majestic, that the simple-minded might easily conclude that Dom Pedro the Second had been deposed, and that he, Sir Knight of the golden side, had been elected to the throne, and only awaited the day of his coronation.

Constantine the Great was not more self-gratulatory, when he saw his dream confirmed by the sign in the heavens, and the sign proved favorable, by his signal victory, than our noble explorer is, to find that the report of his warmly attached friends is literally true: for the country *is* sterile, along that line of Railroad, beyond a doubt.

Mr. Shylock is now paid for the rent of the house, upon which he receives a commission, of course: and Mr. Shylcock is employed to procure passports, &c., all of which "cost, infernally."

"Well, no matter; go on and get them, for they will be the last I will pay the thieving scoundrels for." While Mr. Shylock works the ropes, our honest, indignant traveller is engaged in procuring a few curiosities; such as beetles, set in pinchbeck jewelry; perhaps a monkey, or a parrot. While engaged in these weighty duties, in the midst of the vexatious perplexities consequent upon one man undertaking to accomplish so much; the side-walks of the principal streets being narrow, and our hero large and portly, lo! he is jostled, by a Brazilian citizen of African descent: who presumes to apologize, by raising his hat, and moving politely on. He has scarcely recovered from this rude shock of free-negroism, when he espies, at the very next corner, a man, apparently white, conversing upon terms of perfect equality, with another citizen of the same extraction, as black as can be. Here is proof, positive, of the existence of that hateful thing, 'negro equality,' of which his dear sympathetic friends, Shylock and Go-between, have given him so many harrowing accounts.. In the midst of his burning indignation, he forgets the numerous thefts, rapes, and murders, committed by North American citizens, descended from the same stock, officered by some of the loyal relations of his loving friend Go-between, in his own native State. He forgets how many of the ladies of the South have been violated; and how many refined ladies have been whipped, and scourged, by ladies and gentlemen of color; protected by those who had the power to have prevented such brutal outrages. He forgets those instances in which ladies have been tied before a slow fire, and their feet roasted, to make them disclose the hiding place of the little purse of gold, until the once lithe, and happy creatures, are now club-footed and toeless. He does not remember how his own sisters are afraid to venture out to take an evening walk, lest they should encounter a band of colored marauders, with arms in their hands.

Oh no! He does not remember the pathetic account he gave of all these terrible things, a short time since; for he is now chiefly anxious to return to "the land of the free, and the home of the brave."

In Brazil, where the government is stable, the laws equitable and just; where the smallest infractions of law are inevitably punished; where the inhabitants are so peaceful and honest, that he has not found it necessary to turn a key, to secure his valuables (until recently, some enterprising North American thieves were discovered to be about, and notice was given by the police to hotel keepers to lock up, until they could be caught), he has taken fright at "negro equality;" and proposes to mend the matter, by returning to the land where negro superiority is just now a prevailing mania.

But amid all these disgusting things, he does not forget to note carefully down the valuable information he has obtained; together with Mr. Shylock's and Mr. Go-between's opinion, as to the precise period, in the immediate future, when the institution of slavery in Brazil will cease to exist, and the effete empire become a republic. These last are important, for he intends to talk, and write, prodigiously on his return.

In all this fascinating intercourse, these affectionate attentions, wonderful discoveries, and unerring predictions as to the future of Brazil, there is one thing that has escaped the notice of our mighty investigator. Strange, too, that anything should escape one so erudite, so astute, and so bent upon having "the truth, the whole truth, and nothing but the truth." But it is even so. The thing was overlooked, or neglected; and the unfortunate report has gone forth, which might have had a very different ring, if this one little question had been put, at the proper time, followed up by a few others, that naturally appertain to the subject. It is this: "Why do you, Mr. Shylock, and you, Mr. Go-between, remain in this doomed, and doubly accursed country? You were not born here; and you have both informed me that you are not citizens, and never intend to become citizens. And how is it that you are able to send such large sums of money out of the Empire? If I recollect rightly, you have both informed me, in our delightful intercourse, that you were poor men when you came here. One of you was a carpenter and joiner, without the tools to ply your avocation, or the means to purchase the same: no, not even a second suit of clothes. And yet you inform me, that as time rolled on, and your daughters grew up around you, one of them was married; and the wedding was described, by a correspondent of a Philadelphia paper, as 'marriage in high life.' You have entertained me, most graciously, in your own private residences, which might easily be mistaken for palaces. How did you manage to procure them in this poor, barren, God-forsaken region? Besides, you have informed me that the beastly inhabitants are so abominably lazy, that they never pretend to work. How, then, comes it to pass that Brazil is able to carry on such an immense commerce, chiefly in exports?"

If Mr. Shylock, who claims to be a British subject, and Mr. Go-between, who is a Brother Jonathan, would answer truly, they would be obliged to say: We remain in Brazil, because the country has a delightful climate, inexhaustible sources of wealth, is extremely healthy, and well governed: but chiefly, because it gives us better facilities for amassing fortunes than any other; at the same time, ample protection "for life, liberty, and property." And because the Brazilians are so good natured, and amiable, that they are willing to allow us any price for doing their dirty work. Much of our gains comes easily into our hands, by fleecing green-horns, like yourself: we do not become citizens, because that would entail upon us duties, which we prefer to avoid: and it might happen, that in some of our sharp practice, we should be caught, in which event, our governments are powerful, and their representatives at this court, if properly approached, would no doubt interfere, and make sufficient noise to prevent our being punished. And to sum up: we do not want your poor, half starved, gutted, despoiled, but energetic Southerners to come here: for we can easily foresee, that in a few years you will divide with us what we consider a good thing: therefore, we have arranged this whole affair, beginning away back yonder in New York, with a view to keep you out of the country, and at the same time, cause you to give it a bad name, which will keep your countrymen away: while you are so honest and sincere, in believing the falsehood you propagate, that, like your prototype, who fought to establish the fact that the shield was all gold, when it was half silver, you will expend much gas, a little money, and a great deal of paper and ink, to prove that Brazil is all poor, when it is, in reality, nearly all rich. This you would certainly do, if we did not now undeceive you, by this honest confession of ours: all of which goes to prove how easy a thing it is to deceive and befog the self-sufficient, self-im.

portant, self-conceited, lazy man, who is neither competent, nor willing, to investigate for himself; but quite ready to make a big noise, and send up a terrible *report*, by means of borrowed thunder. And, should he reach home, in his newly acquired character, of a full-fledged author and tourist, without strutting his brains out, will astonish the ignorant, amuse the cultivated, and cause the prudent to resolve to 'bear those ills we have, than fly to others that we know not of.'"

Come, Sir Knight, of the Silver side; give us the results of your investigations, and an account of the manner in which you performed the same. You seem to be a Southron born: and judging from the bronze on your cheeks, the furrows upon your brow, and the premature streaks of gray that stray through your locks, you have seen service. Yes, I was there at the beginning, in the middle scene, and at the finale. I was present at that last memorable roll-call, to take my parole, and that terrible oath, administered in the peculiar dialect of New England, which gives to the letter "r" such a strange nasal twang; of late, so harsh, and disagreeable to the ear of a Southern gentleman. That oath of allegiance—which caused my heart to swell and ache, as doubtless the hearts of Christian martyrs do, when bound to the stake—I put into my pocket;

resolved to keep it, inviolate, until cancelled by another, voluntarily taken, to a government more in keeping with my wishes. After procuring permission to travel, from my new masters, I made the best of my way to the nearest port; and was thankful to find the little Schooner Valiant up for Rio de Janeiro. The captain, who was a kind, good soul, did not scrutinize my seedy gray very closely, nor ask me any disagreeable questions: but received me on board, abating somewhat the regular fare, in consequence of the smallness of my purse.

After sixty days of buffeting with the waves, our little craft entered the matchless harbor of Rio de Janiero. Here I brushed and cleaned my very best, and only suit, and with a heart still aching, but resolved to try, sought the best means of obtaining an interview with the proper official to encourage, or dishearten. I was soon able to reach His excellency Paula Souza, then Minister of Agricultura, who received me more like a friend and equal than my shabby appearance would seem to warrant me in expecting. He bade me accept the hospitality of the Empire, and freely state my wishes. Here I was thrown quite off my balance: for the warmth and brotherly feeling he manifested for our hapless condition, rendered my carefully prepared speech, altogether too cold and formal: so that I was obliged to extemporize from first to last. I succeeded, however, in making him understand that I wished to examine into the Brazilian system of government, with a view to becoming a citizen, and of obtaining the privilege of forming a compact settlement of my countrymen, should things prove favorable. "Certainly," said he, "I will furnish you with free transit to any part of the Empire you wish to examine; and with an engineer and interpreter, who will see that your journeyings cost you nothing." These were such words of encouragement, and offers of assistance, as I was not prepared to expect. A transition so sudden, from my floating grave, which had brought me from the bleak field of battle, where the roar of artillery, the greeting of piercing bullets, rending bayonets, and gashing sabres, had taught me hardness, to the genial sunshine of generous friendliness, offered by a minister of State, had a singular effect, and I was foolish enough to shed tears. No time was lost, however, in getting ready for the contemplated tour. We were off, in a few days, into the northern provinces of Brazil, where we found lands too dear, and in bodies too small to suit our purpose. At every point, we were received in the genuine spirit of hospitality. Some of our entertainments were upon a scale, equally, if not more magnificent than anything of the kind I had ever witnessed. In some of these palatial residences, I saw plate which, while it was more massive than any I had ever seen, reminded me sadly of the dear old heirloom silver, which my darling sister wrote me, long before the surrender, had been torn from her own, and our poor feeble mother's hands, by the gallant officers and men, who finally succeeded, through the assistance of Europe, and Africa, in overrunning and crushing my native South. After some two months of travel in the magnificent coffee regions of North Brazil, and being entertained frequently at fazendas, where the annual income ranges from fifty to one hundred thousand dollars, I returned to the capital, and told His Excellency, the Minister of Agricultura, that while the immense country I had traversed was rich, healthful, and beautiful beyond my powers of description; I had found no body of land that was cheap enough, or sufficiently extensive, to suit our people, as many as would probably wish to settle together.

"Very well," said he, "would you like to go South, or into the interior?" As I had heard something of the richness of the lands in the province of San Paulo, I asked to go South, that I might examine there. After a few days of preparation, we were off again, and steering southward, soon found a delicious climate, a most romantic, thoroughly rich, and beautiful country.

In two months of travel more, I found a region surpassing anything I had expected to find. And, what was of greatest interest to me, most of the land was yet the property of the Imperial government. I here selected, and located, a tract sufficiently large for all of my friends: returned to Rio de Janiero, took out my patent of naturalization, which was given by special act of the chambers, then in session, and decree of the Emperor. I also received a provisional title to the land, with authority to regulate its occupancy, according to the wishes of myself and friends.

I now entered into some special arrangements with the government, with the view of aiding indigent persons, of good character, in emigrating to Brazil; in all of which transactions I acted with an eye single to the best interests of my friends. But judge of my surprise, on being introduced to Sir Knight of the golden side, and other inferior Knights, who had found their way to the capital, but no further, at being informed, that my work was all unconstitutional: that the Minister of Agricultura, although acting under explicit instructions from our large-hearted monarch, had transcended his authority in the arrangements he had entered into with myself; therefore my contracts and concessions were null and void. For all of this, I was exceedingly sorrowful. But when Mr. Shylock, and Mr. Go-between, who are both constitutional lawyers, were quoted to prove that such was the fact; I could, of course, have nothing to say. However, after mature reflection, I have concluded to let my Emperor, and his Ministers of State, take the responsibility of violating the constitution: and I have returned, for the purpose of assisting my friends to emigrate to Brazil.

Sir Knight of the Golden Side says the Empire of Brazil is all poor, because his admirable friends and benefactors, Mr. Shylock, and Mr. Go-between, have told him so: while I, Sir Knight of the Silver Side, do assert, most positively, because I have seen it with mine own eyes, that a very large proportion of Brazil, is immensely rich: and large enough to contain ten such populations as now inhabit the United States, without being too densely peopled. You have the record of each, and the diverse stories that we relate: as also the "reasons for the hope that is in us." Harmonize, if you will; believe both, if you can.

CHAPTER III.

THE GOVERNMENT, THE CONSTITUTION, AND THE LANGUAGE SPOKEN.

The most direct and satisfactory mode of arriving at a correct understanding of the character of a government, is to examine into its organic law; comparing this with the constitutions of other countries, of which we know something; and then inform ourselves as to whether the Constitution is held sacred by the ruling sovereign, and whether the laws enacted by the legislature, and enforced by the people, are in accordance with the same.

To this end, I will here give an abstract of the Brazilian constitution, and a brief account of the estimation in which it is held by the present Emperor, the legislative bodies, and the great mass of the people.

It was my intention to have printed this admirable instrument of government entire; but lack of space must be my apology for offering the following

ABSTRACT
OF THE BRAZILIAN CONSTITUTION,

Sworn to on the 25th of March, 1824, *and revised in* 1834.

(1) BRAZIL is declared an Independent Empire, and its Government Monarchial, Constitutional, and Representative. (2) The Reigning Dynasty is to be Dom Pedro I. and his successors. (3) The Roman Catholic religion is constituted that of the State; but the exercise of all others is permitted. (4) The unrestricted communication of thought, either by means of words, writings, or the agency of the press, exempt from censure, is guaranteed: with the condition that all who abuse this privilege shall become amenable to the law. (5) A guarantee founded on the principles of the English Habeas Corpus Act. (6) The privileges of citizenship are extended to all free natives of Brazil, to all Portuguese resident there from the time of the Independence, and to all naturalized strangers. (7) The law is declared equal to all; all are liable to taxation in proportion to their possessions. (8) The highest offices of the State are all laid open to every citizen; and all privileges, excepting those of office, abolished. (9) The political powers acknowledged by the Constitution are the Legislative,

the Moderative, the Executive, and the Judicial; all of which are acknowledged as delegations from the nation. (10) It is declared that the General Assembly shall consist of two chambers: the Chamber of Deputies are to hold their office for four years only; the Senators are appointed for life (11) The especial attributes of the Assembly are to administer the oaths to the Emperor, the Imperial Prince, the Regent, or the Regency; to elect the Regent or Regency, and to fix the limits of his or their authority; to acknowledge the Imperial Prince as successor to the throne, on the first meeting after his birth; to nominate the guardian of the young Emperor in case such guardian has not been named in the parental testament; to resolve all doubts relative to the succession on the death of the Emperor or vacancy of the throne; to examine into the past administration, and to reform its abuses; to elect a new dynasty in case of the extinction of the reigning family; to pass laws, and also to interpret, suspend, and revoke them; to guard the Constitution, and to promote the welfare of the nation; to fix the public expenditure and taxes; to appoint the marine and land forces annually upon the report of the Government; to concede, or refuse, the entry of foreign forces within the Empire; to authorize the Government to contract loans to establish means for the payment of the public debt; to regulate the administration of national property and decree its alienation; to create or suppress public offices, and to fix the stipend to be allotted to them; and, lastly, to determine the weight, value, inscription, type, and denomination of the coinage.

(12) During the term of their office, the members of both Houses are alike exempted from arrest, unless by the authority of their respective Chambers, or when seized in the commission of a capital offence. For the opinions uttered during the exercise of their functions, they are inviolable. (13) All measures for the levying of imposts and military enrolment, the choice of a new dynasty in case of the extinction of the existing one, the examination of the acts of the past administration, and the accusation of Ministers, and of Councillors of State, are required to have their origin with the House of Deputies. For the idemnification of its members, it is decided that a pecuniary remuneration shall be allotted to each during the period of the sessions. (14) The number of the Senators is fixed at one-half that of the Deputies, and the members are required to be upwards of forty years of age, and to be in actual possession of an income amounting to at least eight hundred milreis per annum. (15) It is their exclusive attribute to take cognizance of the

individual crimes committed by the members of the Imperial Family, Ministers, or Councillors of State, as well as of the crimes of Deputies during the period of the Legislature. Their annual stipend is fixed at fifty per cent. more than that of the Deputies.

(16) The Members of both Chambers are to be chosen by Provincial Electors, who are themselves to be elected by universal suffrage,—in which only minors, monks, domestics, and individuals not in the receipt of one hundred milreis per annum, are excluded from voting. (17) The Senators are nominated by the Provincial Electors in triple lists, from which three candidates the Emperor selects one, who holds office for life. (19) Each Chamber is qualified with powers for the proposition, opposition, and approval of projects of law. In case, however, the House of Deputies should disapprove of the *amendments* or *additions* of the Senate, or *vice versâ*, the dissenting Chamber shall have the privilege of requiring a temporary union of the two Houses, in order that the matter in dispute may be decided in General Assembly.

(20) A *veto* is conceded to the Emperor; but it is only suspensory in its nature. In case three successive Parliaments should present the same project for the Imperial sanction, it is declared that

on the third presentation it shall, under all and any circumstances, be considered that the sanction had been conceded. (21) The ordinary annual sessions of the two Houses of Legislature are limited to the period of four months.

(22) To each province of the Empire there is a legislative Assembly, for the purpose of discussion on its particular interests, and the promotion of projects of law accommodated to its localities and urgencies; but these Assemblies are not invested with any power excepting that of proposing laws of provincial interest.

(23) The attributes of the *moderative power* (which is designated the key to the entire political organization, and which is vested exclusively in the hands of the Emperor) are the nomination of Senators, according to the before-mentioned regulations; the convocation of the General Assembly whenever the good of the Empire shall require it; the sanction of the decrees or resolutions of the Assembly; the enforcement or suspension of the projects of the provincial Assemblies during the recess of the Chambers; the dissolution of the House of Deputies; the nomination of Ministers of State; the suspension of magistrates; the diminution of the penalties imposed on criminals; and the concession of amnesties.

(24) The titles acknowledged in the Constitution as appertaining to His Majesty are "Constitutional Emperor and Perpetual Defender of Brazil." His person is declared inviolable and sacred, and he himself exempt from all responsibility. He is, moreover, designated as the chief of the *executive power*, which power is to be exercised through the medium of his Ministers. Its principal functions are the convocation of a new General Assembly in the third year of each legislature, the nomination of bishops, magistrates, military and naval commanders, ambassadors, and diplomatic and commercial agents; the formation of all treaties of alliance, subsidy, and commerce; the declaration of war and peace; the granting of patents of naturalization, and the exclusive power of conferring titles, military orders, and other honorary distinctions. All acts emanating from the executive power are to be signed by the Ministers of State, before being carried into execution; and those Ministers are to be held responsible for all abuses of power, as well as for treason, falsehood, peculation, or attempts against the liberty of the subjects. (25) In addition to the *Ministry*, a Council of State is also appointed, the members of which are to hold offices for life. They are to be heard concerning all matters of serious import, and principally on all sub-

jects relating to war and peace, negotiations with foreign States, and the exercise of the moderative power. For all counsels wilfully tending to the prejudice of the State, they are to be held responsible.

(26) The *judicial power* is declared independent, and is to consist of judges and juries for the adjudication of both civil and criminal cases, according to the disposition of future codes for this effect. The juries are to decide upon the fact, and the judges to apply the law. For all abuses of power the judges, as well as the other officers of justice, are to be held responsible. It is within the attributes of the Emperor to suspend the judges in the exercise of their functions; but they are to be dismissed from office only by a sentence of the supreme courts of appeal instituted in all the provinces.

(28) The *presidents of the provinces* are to be nominated by the Emperor; but their privileges, qualifications, and authority are to be regulated by the Assembly.

(29) If, after the expiration of four years, it should be found that any articles of the Constitution required reform, it was decreed that the proposed amendment should originate with the House of Deputies; and if, after discussion, the necessity of the reform was conceded, an act was to be passed and sanctioned by the Emperor in the usual man-

ner, requiring the electors of the Deputies for the next Parliament to confer on their representatives especial powers regarding the proposed alteration or reform. On the assembling of the next House of Deputies, the matter in question was to be proposed and discussed, and, if passed, to be appended to the Constitution and solemnly promulgated. (The reforms were few,—the two principal being the regulation of succession in the case of the death of Dom Pedro II. without issue, his sister Donna Januaria, or her children, becoming heirs; and changing the provincial councils to provincial Assemblies.)

(30) Finally, civil and criminal codes are organized; the use of torture is abolished; the confiscation of property is prohibited; the custom of declaring the children and relatives of criminals infamous is abrogated, and the rights of property and the public debt are guaranteed.

The present excellent ruler of Brazil looks upon the great original, (of which this is an abstract,) given by his father to the people, and proclaimed the supreme law of the land, by the unanimous voice of the nation, as the rule, and gauge, of all his official acts. He frequently remarks, in his official intercourse with native statesmen, as also in his interviews with foreigners, who are apt to ask for extraordinary favors, and interferences: "I am a constitutional monarch; and cannot, therefore, go beyond the letter and spirit of the instrument that gave us independence and nationality."

In the Senate, as in the House of Deputies, when any measure is brought forward, it is at once tried by the touchstone of the constitution; if found to accord with that, then it only remains to settle the utility of the law; when it passes, or is rejected, as the majority deem it wholesome, or unwholesome. But, should it be found, in any sense, unconstitutional, no amount of eloquence, or pleading for "higher law," can keep it long before these bodies. All laws, thus enacted, are held sacredly binding by the people: so, that there exists no country under the sun, where the rights of the citizen, and the foreigner, are more happily conserved than in Brazil. The rights of property, as guaranteed in the constitution, are carried out to the letter. The Senator, with the highest title of nobility, does not presume to enter the humblest dwelling, without first asking permission; and should permission be withheld, he does not enter, except at his own peril. This is because the constitution makes every man lord supreme, in his own domicil; however humble or lowly it may be.

Many believe, because they have been told so, by designing knaves, and politicians, who wish to detain them in this country, that foreigners cannot hold property in Brazil; particularly in slaves. This is utterly without foundation. Any foreigner, no matter where he may be from, can hold as many slaves as he is able to buy, or as much property, of any description, as he is able to pay for.

The laws are open to all, and a foreigner stands as good a chance to get justice in the courts, as if he had been born in the Empire. But happily for the people, there is but little litigation going on in the country.

I know a Massachusetts Yankee, who refuses to be naturalized, and yet he owns several slaves. I know many southern gentlemen, who have bought large numbers of slaves, and much real estate, during the last year.

I hope these instances will quiet the apprehensions of the over credulous and timid, on these points.

The next thing to be noticed, is the popular error that exists in the United States, as to the ancestors of the Brazilians, and the language they speak, and write. I have been greatly amused, since my return, at the talkative ignorance, and pretentious manners, of many, who have undertaken to catechise me on the subject of Brazil. One United States Senator, was particularly confident, and assuming. He opened the conversation, by asserting, in a knowing and suggestive tone, "Government despotic, of course." "Oh no," said I, "on the contray; very free, and just." "Why," replied he, "have not they an *Emperor*? And of course, where an Emperor rules, the government is despotic." To this master stroke of logic, which seems to be the style just now in vogue, in this country, I made no reply. Finding me dumb, he thought it needful that my pride, and folly, should be a little futher humbled; so he resumed the subject, with all the assurance of success, that a New England Pedagogue feels, when he undertakes to prove to his attentive pupils that Plymouth Rock is the most sacred and hallowed spot on earth. "Then," said he, rather sharply, "you think the government of Brazil is not despotic. How can it be otherwise? when it is composed of such Spaniards, and their descendants, as wish to continue, in the new world, the same despotic forms of government that curse the old." "Hold a moment," said I, "you talk very learnedly, to all appearances; and doubtless, your logic would prove conclusive, with such as you are accustomed to harangue. But, as for myself, I must beg leave to reject it; at the same time, I take the liberty of informing you, that your conclusions are as false, as the premises you have assumed." "Oh!" said he, "what then?" My reply was, "I will tell you; if you will permit me to state a few facts, that I know to be such, from personal observation, and personal experience. In the first place, the Brazilians are not Spaniards, nor the descendants of Spaniards. They are descended from the Portuguese, who discovered the country, colonized it, and held it, until, under Dom Pedro the First, son of Dom John, the Sixth of Portugal, the Colonies declared for independence, and won it: under the glorious constitution, that has since been so dear to the heart of every Brazilian, and the admiration of the first statesmen of the nineteenth century, in both hemispheres. So far from being Spaniards, or in any way mixed up with Spaniards, the Brazilians despise that treacherous race; and point to Mexico, Central America, and the South American republics, when they would warn their sons against the folly, villainy, and insecure character of republicanism. If an intelligent Brazilian who loves liberty and security, and can appreciate good government, were asked what he most abhors, he would doubtless answer, "Spanish American Republicanism." They are intensely national, and loyal to the constitution, and the throne; while they have a just pride in the Portuguese language, their mother tongue, which is the elder daughter of the Latin, and boasts a literature, second, only, to that of the French, among the descendants of the Romans.

CHAPTER IV.

LIZZIELAND: OR THE LOCALITY CHOSEN FOR OUR SETTLEMENT.

After much laborious travel and investigation, I chose for our settlement, a tract of country forty miles long, and twenty-four miles wide. This survey contains 614,000 acres; which, however, is not all government land. Many of the river fronts are claimed by Brazilians, who now occupy them. In every instance, these proprietors evince a disposition to sell out, at very low prices; so that those of our people who desire river fronts, have only to satisfy themselves that the titles are good, when they can purchase, in most instances, as cheaply as if the land belonged to the government. They are willing to sell thus cheaply, because their lands have cost them little or nothing. According to a law of the Empire, enacted to protect squatters, their homesteads have come into their possession by occupancy, not purchase. And as they are not agriculturalists, but desirous of seeing such as cultivate the soil settle in the country, they offer to sell, and remove to regions more remote from civilization. If it be asked why I did not select lands that belong exclusively to the government; the reply is, because no lands of this kind are to be found, in localities that are easy of access. The region selected is the most fertile, healthful, and accessible that I could find; and at the same time, least encumbered with squatters. In fact, I do not regard the few private claims within our survey, (perhaps not a twentieth part of the whole,) as any disadvantage whatever; for, as I have before stated, they can be bought quite as cheaply as the government rates. This I know to be the fact, for I purchased for my own homestead one of the best tracts of land on the Juquiá River, at less than the government price. This tract is what we term the "central residence," or nucleus of the proposed settlement. There are buildings enough already erected to shelter, temporarily, some two hundred persons; where the ladies and children can remain, while the husbands and brothers are selecting suitable sites for plantations, and putting up such buildings as the time and circumstances may seem to justify. This survey, or Lizzieland, as it is now called, lies along the Juquiá River; with a strip four miles wide on one side, and the main body, or a tract twenty miles wide, on the other. To follow the meanderings of the river, through the entire survey, which is forty miles long, I suppose the distance would be near one hundred miles. The river is navigable for steamboats, of four feet draught, about half way through the entire tract; there, the navigation is interrupted by an immense fall, where there is water-power sufficient to turn half the spindles of Manchester. Above this fall, the stream widens out, and is only navigable for canoes and small boats. But below the lower line of the survey, there comes into the Juquiá River a beautiful stream that flows almost through the centre of the main tract: this stream is also navigable for twenty miles, for the largest kind of pirogues, thus giving abundance of water navigation, which is of first importance to a planting people. Besides these streams, there are creeks and springs to be found all over the country, at convenient distances for residences; so that I feel justified in asserting that there is no region in the world better watered than this. And, as to the quality of the water, it is not too much to say, that it is as pure as ice, clear as crystal, and quite cool enough to be palatable, whether you dip it from the spring, the creek, or the river. The land is not heavily, but well timbered. That is, I believe there is timber enough for all practical purposes, of the very best and most durable qualities; while the same amount of labor that it requires to prepare one acre for the plow in the Mississippi bottom, would prepare three times that amount, as a general thing, throughout this entire region. The soil is very fertile, and also very friendly to cultivate. For a more extended description of the country, see my official report Nó. 2, in Chapter X.

The following is a literal translation from the Portuguese, of the terms upon which this land has been given into my hands.

RIO DE JANEIRO, *June* 30, 1866.

DIRECTORY OF PUBLIC LANDS.

By order of His Excellency, The Minister of Agriculture, I have to declare to Rev. Ballard S. Dunn, the following:

1st. The price of the land selected, is one real per square braca, (footing up forty-one and three-quarter cents per acre,) inclusive of the expenses of measuring and marking.

2d. The quantity of land that each emigrant can take, will be regulated by him, and the said

Rev. Ballard S. Dunn, who will be held responsible for the respective payments to the government.

3d. The lands being selected, the said Rev. Ballard S. Dunn will receive a provisional title, clearly indicating the respective limits; this title will be exchanged for another definite one of the property, so soon as the value of the lands occupied is paid into the treasury.

4th. All implements of agriculture, manufactures, machines, and utensils which the emigrants bring with them, for their own use, will be exempt from import duties.

5th. The government will immediately make provisional housing, for the reception of the emigrants.

6th. As to transport, the government will pay the freightage of one vessel, for every two vessels freighted by Rev. Ballard S. Dunn, and bringing emigrants; or will advance the cost of the passage of such emigrants, after their arrival in Brazil, the said gentleman (Dunn) becoming responsible for the reimbursement of the money within the term of three to four years. This responsibility will be made effective by a mortgage of the lands that he may purchase in the Empire.

7th. The emigrants will be able to disembark at Iguape, without passing through Rio de Janeiro, if the government receives a communication, through the intermediacy of the Brazilian consul, or vice consul, of their coming, in a mode to afford time to transmit orders for that purpose, seeing that said port has no custom house.

God have you in care.

[Signed]

BERNARDO AUGUSTO NACENTE AZAMBUJA.

REVERENDO, BALLARD S. DUNN.

The provisional title, of which the above terms speak, I have received, and now have it in my possession; so that I am looked upon in that country, as the legitimate controller of the land. The government has given, in the most public manner, explicit orders, that no one can settle there without my permission, as the land is specially set apart for myself and friends.

You see, also, from the above, that I have no compensation from the government, for the labors and the responsibility they have seen fit to impose; beyond the right to select the people with whom we expect to cast our lot in the future. From this source, however, I hope to derive the richest compensation. If, after weighing well all

3

the circumstances, good men and women come to the conclusion that the best thing they can do, is to expatriate themselves, then, surely, it behooves them to see to it, that their new surroundings shall be equally desirable with those they leave behind: otherwise, where lies the advantage of emigrating? The Brazilian form of government, just, stable, and desirable as it is, will be but poor compensation for all the toils and vexations of an expensive removal, if we are to be surrounded by adventurers, who leave their country for their country's good: by restless, unprincipled creatures, who seek new communities because, for a time, they can there practise the same villainies for which they were obliged to remove. Nor are we anxious to welcome those who flee from internal revenue stamps, and direct taxation, from the same principle that they dodged Confederate conscript officers, made out false returns of able-bodied negroes, or detailed fifteen hands to one son, a ferryboat to another, and a corn mill to a third, to keep them out of the army. Such men are not desirable as friends, nor to be dignified by the name of foes. We want honest, virtuous, brave people; who do always what they believe to be right, from high principle, and are not ashamed of their record, disastrous though it has been. Such people, no matter how poor they may find themselves, shall be of us, and ours, if it be their desire. In a community formed of such materials, the little form by which I have already received several noble souls, would not be out of place. It reads as follows:

"This welcomes Mr. A. into Lizzieland, a community to be formed of such expatiated Southerners, from the United States, as will continue in force among themselves, we humbly trust, that law of honor, and Christian rectitude, which obviates the necessity for enforcing any other law. It is intended to make this community as compact as possible, for planting purposes, at the same time allowing ample room for the largest planters." In order to carry out these intentions fully, I have stipulated that the land shall be surveyed into sections of six hundred and forty acres each. The young man who wishes no more than six hundred and forty acres, can enter that amount: those of larger families, and greater ability to cultivate, can take more, until the amount reaches a reasonable apportionment; say three sections. In no case, however, will persons be permitted to enter land with a view to speculation, merely, within this tract. That our lands will grow valuable most rapidly, we are very sanguine. But this increase of value will be legitimate, and in no sense detrimental to the general good. In fact, I look upon this, as one of the great points gained by my exertions. By our presence there, we will mutually enrich each other; while our gain will be no one's loss; for the Brazilian government gives us the land at legal rates, and will be as happy as we, to see it grow in value; and are even now saying, as the lord of those servants in the parable of the talents, "to him that hath, shall be given." I have been assured by the leading men of the Empire, that we need have no fears for the future, once we get started, on the score of government aid, in carrying out any public works, that we shall find necessary. From Ballard, the central residence, on the Juquiá River, the government is now surveying a road, that is to be finished at once, a distance of twelve miles into the interior, through the choicest of the lands; which will cost about fifty thousand dollars. It is to be a good eighteen feet track, well thrown up, with the timber cleared seventy feet; with bridges that are to be secure for the heaviest wagons. The contract to construct this road had been guaranteed to one of our countrymen, in whose energy and ability, we have great confidence; who holds my power of attorney to act in such matters, during my absence from the Empire. The government also gives five thousand dollars per annum, towards the steam navigation of the Ribeira River and its tributaries. I hope to find that this same gentleman has placed a steamer on the river by the time we return; so that when we leave the ship at Iguape, we can go on board our own steamer, and ascend the Ribeira and Juquiá Rivers, to our future homes. And I now invite all, into whose hands this book may fall, between this and the 15th of March, 1867, who can, and are willing to give satisfactory references, to communicate with me, at New Orleans, on the subject of emigrating to Brazil. State how many there are in the family, the ages and condition of all; whether they wish to pay their own passage, or whether they wish to accept the aid offered by the government; in the way of a loan for four years. It is my intention to sail from New Orleans, about the last days of March next: direct for the town of Iguape, on the coast of Brazil, about four hundred miles south of Rio de Janeiro. It will be necessary to know who is going, how many, and upon what conditions, at least fifteen days in advance, in order to make preparations accordingly. If enough conclude to go at that time, to load three comfortable ships, with passengers and their necessary freight, I purpose accepting the first terms offered by the government:

that is, that we pay the charter of *two* ships, the government paying the charter of the *third*. This is a more simple arrangement, and entails less responsibility upon me. Besides, I think *one* to *two*, will meet the necessities of all the worthy indigent persons who will want to emigrate. But should this not be the case, and enough of men of means conclude to go, we will charter a good double-decker steamer, and go quickly and comfortably. And, should any worthy person, of either sex, wish to accept the government loan, I will be happy, indeed, in assuming the responsibility, and take them along.

CHAPTER V.

THE WEATHER—ITS TEMPERATURE.

THE following statement of the weather, was kept for one year, from December 1, 1859, to December 1, 1860, by Mr. Jacob Humbid, at Brandon, on the Dom Pedro Segunda Railroad, about forty miles interior from Rio de Janiero. This gentleman, as I have elsewhere stated, is the contractor to whom Brazil is indebted for the successful completion of a large portion of that gigantic undertaking. I am able, through his politeness and thoughtfulness, to place before our people, a table for one year, that exhibits a temperature very similar to that of our chosen locality, in the Province of San Paulo; except that it is slightly warmer, with a climate a little drier.

In all my journeyings in the Empire of Brazil, I never found the heat oppressive by day, nor any thing but pleasant by night. In fact, for the greater portion of the year, in the Province of San Paulo, the nights are so delightfully cool, that considerable cover is necessary, in order to sleep comfortably. This, to one who has roasted in the excessive heat of Charleston, Mobile, New Orleans, and Galveston; or upon the prairies of Texas, and the plains of Mexico, was an agreeable surprise.

THERMOMETER AND WEATHER ACCOUNT FOR ONE YEAR.

DECEMBER, 1859.

	6 A. M.	12 M.	6. P. M.	REMARKS.
1	80°	84°	77°	9 a. m. 88° ; 2 p. m. rain.
2	74	75	73	rain.
3	67	71	71	rain.
4	70	73	73	cloudy ; 6 p. m. rain.
5	72	78	76	" " " "
6	72	89	76	variable ; 12½ rain.
7	72	81	76	" " "
8	73	75	73	rain.
9	71	73	72	showery.
10	69½	73	69	rain.
11	64	69	63	variable ; 2 p. m. rain.
12	63	72	72	" 3 p. m. ther. 76°
13	61	76	76	clear ; 4 p. m. " 73°
14	72	79	74	variable.
15	72	74	72	"
16	64	72	73	"
17	68	76	72	" 2 p. m. rain.
18	66	76	72	clear.
19	69	77	74	variable.
20	70	76	74	"
21	68	76	73	"
22	71	76	79	"
23	74	79	76	cloudy.
24	72	74	73	" forenoon rain.
25	74	76	80	variable.
26	74	76	74	rain.
27	72	74	70	"
28	68	74	73	variable.
29	68	80	76	"
30	68	72	73	cloudy.
31	68	74	72	rain.

JANUARY, 1860.

	6 A. M.	12 M.	6 P. M.	REMARKS.
1	68°	74°	72°	cloudy and rainy.
2	72	76	74	" 3 p. m. rain.
3	70	76	78	variable.
4	74	77	74	cloudy; 3 p. m. rain.
5	64	68	68	" and rainy.
6	88	74	74	variable.
7	72	80	76	clear.
8	74	80	84	"
9	73	81	85	"
10	74	80	84	"
11	74	82	86	"
12	75	82	87	"
13	76	86	88	"
14	78	84	86	"
15	76	84	88	"
16	78	82	86	cloudy.
17	76	84	86	"
18	74	80	76	6 p. m. rain.
19	70	74	76	" .. "
20	72	76	72	rain.
21	74	78	73	variable.
22	74	80	80	"
23	74	81	84	"
24	76	79	72	cloudy and rainy.
25	73	78	74	" "
26	78	74	76	cloudy.
27	72	82	83	clear.
28	76	85	83	ther. 3 p. m. 90°.
29	78	88	83	clear.
30	76	84	85	"
31	76	84	80	"

FEBRUARY, 1860.

	6 A. M.	12 M.	6 P. M.	REMARKS.
1	74°	83°	80°	clear.
2	76	82	78	cloudy.
3	75	87	80	variable.
4	76	88	82	cloudy; 4 p.m. rain; 2 th.91°.
5	76	82	86	cloudy and rainy.
6	75	81	78	cloudy.
7	75	78	80	" and rainy.
8	74	80	80	" "
9	72	80	82	cloudy.
10	74	82	84	"
11	76	84	86	"
12	76	86	80	"
13	74	80	76	4 p. m. rain.
14	74	81	78	5 " "
15	74	82	79	"
16	74	82	80	clear; ther. 3 p. m. 84°.
17	74	82	84	" " 4 " 86°.
18	75	84	80	cloudy; 5 p. m. rain.
19	76	86	84	"
20	76	84	86	clear; ther. 4 p. m. 89°.
21	78	89	90	" " 3 " 92°.
22	80	90	86	variable.
23	79	84	76	cloudy; 1 p. m. rain.
24	72	73	71	" and rainy.
25	68	71	70	"
26	67	74	72	"
27	70	76	80	variable.
28	74	80	76	cloudy and rainy.
29	74	80	78	"
30				
31				

MARCH, 1860.

	6 A. M.	12 M.	6 P. M.	REMARKS.
1	74°	78°	76°	cloudy and rainy.
2	74	78	80	"
3	72	84	86	clear.
4	76	74	76	" ther. 4 p. m. 89°.
5	78	84	88	"
6	78	90	86	"
7	78	87	86	"
8	76	86	84	"
9	78	86	88	" ther. 4 p. m. 90°.
10	80	91	90	"
11	82	88	90	" " 3 " 92°.
12	80	88	90	" " " " 93°.
13	82	88	86	cloudy.
14	78	89	78	" and rainy.
15	76	82	78	rain.
16	78	81	80	cloudy.
17	76	83	76	"
18	78	84	78	rain.
19	76	84	80	cloudy.
20	76	82	78	"
21	76	88	80	clear.
22	78	86	78	cloudy; 5 p. m. rain.
23	70	74	72	rain.
24	70	72	69	"
25	68	72	72	"
26	70	76	73	cloudy.
27	70	84	80	" 4 p. m. rain.
28	73	84	82	cloudy.
29	78	88	86	variable.
30	76	88	86	clear.
31	75	86	84	"

APRIL, 1860.

	6 A. M.	12 M.	6 P. M.	REMARKS.
1	76°	84°	80°	variable.
2	76	85	84	clear.
3	78	88	84	cloudy.
4	78	89	80	"
5	78	89	78	cloudy and rainy.
6	74	80	79	clear.
7	76	84	82	"
8	78	86	86	" ther. 3 p. m. 90°.
9	78	86	84	"
10	74	86	86	"
11	74	88	80	cloudy.
12	72	82	78	"
13	74	84	84	clear.
14	73	86	80	"
15	72	82	78	"
16	72	84	80	"
17	72	82	84	"
18	74	86	86	"
19	78	80	88	"
20	76	80	78	cloudy and rainy.
21	70	76	74	"
22	72	80	74	variable.
23	72	80	76	rain.
24	88	70	68	"
25	67	74	74	variable.
26	69	80	78	"
27	74	78	76	clear.
28	71	80	78	"
29	74	79	78	"
30	74	78	76	cloudy.

MAY, 1860.

	6 A. M.	12 M.	6 P. M.	REMARKS.
1	74°	79°	76	cloudy.
2	72	80	78	" and rainy.
3	72	80	76	"
4	74	84	78	"
5	74	86	80	"
6	74	74	72	rain.
7	74	74	72	"
8	70	70	72	"
9	69	66	67	"
10	65	65	64	"
11	65	68	67	"
12	68	72	68	cloudy.
13	68	72	67	clear.
14	64	72	68	"
15	66	74	66	"
16	66	68	64	rain.
17	64	70	74	clear.
18	64	72	73	"
19	62	74	70	"
20	61	74	71	"
21	65	80	78	"
22	78	80	78	"
23	79	86	84	"
24	78	85	82	"
25	78	84	80	"
26	74	80	78	"
27	70	81	76	cloudy.
28	70	72	70	rain.
29	68	74	73	clear.
30	68	76	70	"
31	68	70	73	"

JUNE, 1860.

	6 A. M.	12 M.	6. P. M.	REMARKS.
1	68°	80°	76°	clear.
2	70	82	78	"
3	72	76	82	cloudy.
4	70	74	75	"
5	72	76	73	"
6	67	74	72	clear.
7	68	76	74	"
8	64	76	74	"
9	72	82	78	"
10	68	74	68	cloudy.
11	64	72	70	"
12	62	78	65	clear.
13	68	75	72	cloudy.
14	69	76	74	"
15	72	74	74	"
16	74	79	72	"
17	72	78	74	rain.
18	68	70	70	clear.
19	68	78	74	cloudy.
20	70	80	78	" and rainy.
21	70	76	72	"
22	71	76	74	variable.
23	70	71	68	clear.
24	65	68	64	"
25	55	68	70	"
26	59	72	71	"
27	62	74	72	"
28	66	76	74	"
29	66	74	72	"
30	66	76	74	cloudy.

JULY, 1860.

	6 A. M.	12 M.	6 P. M.	REMARKS.
1	68°	72°	70°	variable.
2	60	72	68	"
3	64	72	68	cloudy.
4	68	74	72	variable.
5	68	73	72	cloudy.
6	70	74	70	"
7	68	71	70	clear.
8	60	88	70	variable.
9	64	74	71	"
10	68	72	70	cloudy.
11	60	64	65	rain.
12	62	64	64	"
13	64	72	70	clear.
14	68	76	74	"
15	72	80	79	" ther. 3 p. m. 82°.
16	72	79	80	"
17	70	81	80	"
18	70	80	78	"
19	68	80	79	"
20	70	70	69	cloudy.
21	70	68	64	"
22	66	78	74	clear.
23	66	78	76	"
24	70	80	78	cloudy.
25	68	72	70	"
26	66	74	70	"
27	64	74	68	clear.
28	68	80	76	"
29	68	78	74	cloudy.
30	68	76	72	clear.
31	66	74	72	cloudy.

AUGUST, 1860.

	6 A. M.	12 M.	6 P. M.	REMARKS.
1	68°	74°	74°	clear.
2	68	80	78	"
3	72	81	88	"
4	74	86	84	" ther. 3 p. m. 85°.
5	75	88	84	cloudy.
6	70	78	74	clear.
7	70	78	74	cloudy.
8	66	64	62	"
9	64	74	72	rain.
10	68	76	72	cloudy.
11	72	79	78	clear; ther. 3 p. m. 82°.
12	70	80	78	"
13	72	81	78	"
14	70	78	74	cloudy.
15	70	76	72	" and rainy.
16	69	77	74	clear.
17	70	80	78	"
18	74	82	80	"
19	78	80	78	cloudy.
20	72	78	79	"
21	73	80	76	" and rainy.
22	72	79	78	clear.
23	68	70	71	"
24	70	76	78	cloudy and rainy.
25	72	80	78	"
26	72	82	78	"
27	72	80	78	"
28	72	84	78	"
29	72	82	78	"
30	74	80	78	cloudy; ther. 3 p. m. 84°.
31	74	82	78	cloudy.

SEPTEMBER, 1860.

	6 A. M.	12 M.	6 P. M.	REMARKS.
1	74°	84°	82°	clear.
2	70	74	72	cloudy.
3	70	80	76	"
4	68	78	76	"
5	69	82	80	clear; ther. 3 p. m. 84°.
6	72	82	80	variable; ther. 2 p. m. 84°.
7	72	80	78	cloudy.
8	70	78	74	" and rainy.
9	70	76	74	cloudy.
10	68	74	70	"
11	68	70	70	rain.
12	66	70	71	cloudy.
13	70	71	70	"
14	65	68	66	rain.
15	66	70	71	cloudy.
16	74	82	80	clear.
17	70	78	74	cloudy.
18	70	76	74	" and rainy.
19	70	70	70	rain.
20	68	72	70	"
21	70	76	72	cloudy.
22	73	82	78	clear.
23	72	74	70	cloudy and rainy.
24	68	76	72	clear.
25	65	78	74	"
26	74	80	80	" and rainy.
27	72	76	74	"
28	71	80	70	" and rainy.
29	70	80	76	" "
30	72	88	78	" "

OCTOBER, 1860.

	6 A. M.	12 M.	6 P. M.	REMARKS.
1	74°	82°	78°	cloudy; ther. 5 p. m. 84°.
2	74	82	80	clear.
3	76	78	74	cloudy.
4	69	78	76	rain.
5	65	66	64	"
6	66	76	74	cloudy.
7	68	78	76	variable.
8	70	80	76	"
9	69	82	78	clear.
10	68	80	78	cloudy.
11	67	80	76	clear.
12	66	78	74	cloudy.
13	68	76	74	clear.
14	68	80	76	"
15	70	78	76	" ther. 3 p. m. 90°.
16	80	90	78	variable.
17	74	76	68	rain.
18	70	84	72	"
19	70	80	74	variable.
20	76	86	84	clear.
21	78	88	86	"
22	78	89	82	variable.
23	74	88	84	clear.
24	78	89	82	"
25	78	99	80	cloudy.
26	76	76	76	rain.
27	72	74	72	"
28	71	78	74	cloudy.
29	72	82	78	" 5 p. m. rain.
30	74	83	81	"
31	74	82	76	" 4 p. m. rain.

NOVEMBER, 1860.

	6 A. M.	12 M.	6 P. M.	REMARKS.
1	78°	82°	79°	cloudy.
2	78	83	76	" 3 p. m. rain.
3	72	74	72	"
4	71	74	72	cloudy.
5	69	78	76	clear.
6	68	84	80	"
7	76	82	81	" ther. 4 p. m. 88°.
8	78	84	76	cloudy; 5 p. m. rain.
9	68	63	64	rain.
10	64	64	65	"
11	68	75	68	cloudy.
12	70	74	76	clear.
13	71	84	85	"
14	74	74	68	rain.
15	69	72	68	clear.
16	64	76	72	"
17	78	82	80	variable.
18	74	78	76	cloudy.
19	72	76	74	rain.
20	72	88	76	cloudy.
21	76	82	80	"
22	73	83	76	" 2 p. m. rain
23	73	73	72	" " "
24	70	76	74	cloudy.
25	72	82	80	" 6 p. m. rain.
26	75	84	80	cloudy.
27	76	84	80	"
28	76	85	81	2 p. m. rain.
29	78	82	76	cloudy.
30	74	82	80	"

CHAPTER VI.

The following letters, addressed to myself, under the dates they severally bear, are thought to contain information that will prove acceptable to many.

Mr. Demaret, is a native of Louisiana, but for the last eleven years, a resident of Texas. He and his interesting family, had arrived in Brazil, but a short time before I left Rio de Janiero, to return to the United States.

Dr. R. M. Davis, is a Virginian, but for the last eight years, a resident of Brazil. He stands high as a physician, and a man of practical sense; so that his opinions upon the subjects of his letter, are regarded by those who know him as valuable.

Capt. W. Frank Shippey, was an officer of our late navy, and stands deservedly high with all who know him. He is now engaged in opening a plantation on the Ribeira River, in the Province of San Paulo.

RIO DE JANEIRO, *August* 24, 1866.

REV. BALLARD S. DUNN:

DEAR SIR: Having lately returned from the Province of San Paulo, and learning that you are about to sail for the United States, I wish to express my entire approbation of the climate and soil which you have selected for our countrymen in that province. I shall be glad if you will say to my friends and relatives in Texas and Louisiana, that I have already seen enough of Brazil to convince me that my removal to this country was a fortunate one; and that I am now engaged in selecting the best from the best. I am in more robust health than I have been in ten years past. My family are also in excellent health and spirits.

Respectfully, your obedient servant,

M. F. DEMARET.

BARRA DE JUGUIÁ, *June* 2, 1866.

REV. BALLARD S. DUNN,
RIO DE JANEIRO:

DEAR SIR: The hearts of all true Confederates, in this, the exile's home, have been gladdened by the news of the success of your efforts in behalf of our people, and we earnestly pray God that you may be spared to return to us, accompanied by many of our true Southern friends, in order that we, their predecessors, may be able to welcome to our new South, those who shall determine to leave the scenes of their childhood and once happy homes, to emigrate to the hospitable shores of Brazil.

Since the surrender of our armies, I have roamed in exile, over the fairest portions of the globe, but it has been reserved for me to find in Brazil that peace which we all, from sad experience, know so well how to appreciate. Here, the war worn soldier, the bereaved parent, the oppressed patriot, the homeless and despoiled, can find a refuge from the trials which beset them, and a home not haunted by the eternal remembrance of harrowing scenes of sorrow and of death.

This portion of Brazil, I firmly believe, to a greater extent than any other, offers inducements to emigrants, and in particular, to those of our unfortunate countrymen, whose feelings or interests render a longer stay in the Southern States, undesirable or impracticable, while the liberal policy of the government, the equity of its laws, the climate, soil, and vast resources of these hitherto unexplored lands, promises fair to reward the efforts of the settler with wealth and prosperity, while their social relations can be maintained without fear of intrusion or arrest.

We, the advance-guard of the legion of Confederates, who are hereafter to settle and cultivate the soil, watching, as we do, with painful solicitude, the condition of our friends in our late home, earnestly and fondly look for the consummation of your plans and efforts, and I believe that I express the sentiments of all the good and true, when I say that the prayers of the people are with you, and that the children and children's children of those who join our standard, under your auspices, will rise up to call you blessed.

Permit me to reiterate the professions of sincere regard which we all entertain for you, and of the confidence which we repose in your ability, and in the rectitude of your intentions, and wishing you a pleasant and prosperous voyage to the United States, and a safe and speedy return to Brazil.

I remain your friend and obedient servant,

W. FRANK SHIPPEY.

RIO DE JANEIRO, *June* 28, 1866.

REV. BALLARD S. DUNN.

DEAR SIR: You requested me to give you my opinion as to fitness of climate, soil, and productions of San Paulo, for the settlement of our Southern people. I will answer your request as concisely as possible. Within the last six months, I have taken great interest in ascertaining if this country would furnish suitable homes for Southern people, and I am conscientious in saying, that I do not believe that they can be better suited on the globe, than here. All the productions of the Southern States may be raised here, in as great abundance, and with less labor, than in the Southern States at any former period of their history. Corn may be raised in full as great quantity (per acre), and with less labor, and were the same mode of cultivation used, I believe that it would be greater than any of the Southern corn-growing regions. Rice grows here most luxuriantly in every portion of this Province, and yields abundant harvests, even under the rude culture which it receives. With proper cultivation and suitable seed, the crop would surpass any of the Southern States. Cotton grows here finely, matures perfectly, and is of good quality. From what I have seen of the cotton of this Province, growing and matured, I do not think that the very best cotton lands in the Southern States can produce the same quantity (per acre); besides, two crops may be raised from the same planting within thirteen months. Tobacco may be raised profitably in all

4

parts of the Province, to compete favorably with any tobacco-growing country. In fact, I do not believe that this plant could be raised in the United States, if it received no better cultivation there than here. Sugar-cane also grows here to the greatest perfection, and I have been assured by experienced Southern planters, that it grows, matures, and contains more saccharine matter than in the Southern States, and that they can raise at least one third more sugar here, than in those States. I have travelled through different portions of the Province of San Paulo, and have seen all of these crops growing and matured, and have no hesitation in saying, that I do not believe that the United States can compete with this Province in cheapness and quantity, per acre, in any of the articles which I have mentioned, and when our people shall come and settle here, and use their modes of cultivation, there is no country that can yield them greater remuneration for their labor. The water is plentiful and pure as the mountain spring. The climate is excellent and perfectly healthy.

I congratulate you, after your long travels through different portions of the Empire, for the lands which you have chosen, and which have been ceded to you by the government for the

Southern people who may emigrate to this Province. Those lands on the Ribeira and Juquiá Rivers, are of the very best quality. Location healthy, and having the very best water navigation, from your immediate homes, down these rivers to the open sea. This large body of land, rich in soil, with such facilities for transportation, make it one of the most desirable localities I have seen for a large number of emigrants. There they may find a large and fertile tract of country, and as cheap as one could desire, where large numbers may settle, and have an entire community of their own. There they may raise all Southern productions in great abundance, with but little labor, and where they may have a cheap and good transportation for their produce, to the capital of the Empire (one of the best markets in the world). One might travel through this vast Empire, and I do not believe that they could find a country more suited to the wants of the Southern people, than those in which you have been so fortunate in selecting, and I do hope that your untiring perseverance in behalf of the Southern people, may be rewarded by thousands of them coming to this land, where they may enjoy all the free privileges which a brave, but oppressed people may desire, and live at ease and in plenty, where there is no one to oppress them for the expession of "free thought." The climate, soil, and productions of San Paulo, must make it the great nucleus for Southern emigrants to this Empire, and after seeing the different parts of this Province, I am of the opinion that the lands which you have selected afford facilities and conveniences unsurpassed, that make it one of the very best locations that could have been selected for the Southern emigrants. Wishing you much reward for your untiring exertions in behalf of our Southern friends, I remain, very truly yours, &c.

R. M. Davis, M.D.

CHAPTER VII.

SKETCHES TAKEN ON THE GROUND.

THE casual observer of the small group of Americans now assembled in the capital of Brazil, would be likely to dismiss them as the insignificant first fruits of an emigration that must soon end in nothing. But in this conclusion, he would be greatly mistaken. For, in that small, but diverse company, may be found many of the grades of intellect, and shades of temper, common to the race.

The patriotic lovers of their late companions in arms, and unfortunate kindred, are entitled to our first attention. They come and go, in a business like manner; making the most of the golden opportunities offered by a generous government, for discovering, and securing, suitable lands and climates for those they seek to benefit. At every turn, they meet with the most cordial hospitality, and are greeted, with that pleasing civility, and polished politeness, for which the Brazilians are proverbial. In return for such favors, they offer grateful acknowledgments, are thankful and hopeful.

The energetic, money-making, money-loving planter, who did all he could to avert our disasters, but cannot brook the present state of things in the South, chiefly because the labor system is deranged, and insecure, and therefore unfruitful of the golden harvest of former times, has his representative in Rio de Janiero. On the subject of a reliable system of labor, he has grown morbid. He looks for some token of permanency in the present system of Brazil, but is unable to find it. On the contrary, he reads more fearful symptoms of disruption, and violent change, in the politic report of a minister of state, than he was ever able to discover, in the fanatical speeches, and incendiary books, of those who destroyed the South, from John Quincy Adams, down to the emancipation proclamation. For, in those days, "cotton was king;" and under a ruler so potent, he could bask in the perpetual sunshine of conscious security.

That low class of politicians, who prated so much about patriotism, at the commencement of the war, but lacked the ability and the courage necessary to attain distinction in the field; who generally occupied the position of commandants of interior post towns; figured as conscript officers, or quarter master's clerks, have their representatives on the big peninsula. They found it easier to dub themselves majors, colonels, and generals, on arriving here, than to obtain the written commissions corresponding to these ranks, from Mr. Davis. One of these characters, perhaps the highest in rank, that has yet arrived, being an "illustrious General," happened to steam into the port of Rio de Janeiro, on the very crest of the popular wave of American emigration. His staff was almost as numerous as General Magruder's, after the retaking of Galveston. He entered at once upon a career of unparalleled prosperity. But like the small hen, that undertook to hatch seven dozen of eggs at once, he, in attempting to represent seven states, spread himself too much; and, as in the case of poor yarrico, made a mess of it; accompanied by a disagreeable odor, that lingers still in the Brazilian metropolis, very much to the discredit of Southerners.

Following in the footsteps of a flexible predecessor of the same class, who applied to President Jackson for an important appointment, but being refused, concluded to accept a suit of old clothes, our Southron, of the overshadowing rank, numerous staff, and two kinds of aids, consented to accept Irish promotion, in the way of a free passage from the scene of his failure, and a small office in his native land, without rank, and no very great emoluments.

That base order of adventurers, whose love of excitement, and something new, insured them a representation in almost every regiment, at the beginning of the war; who delight in being mistaken, for men of probity and enterprise, have their representatives in the land of the Southern Cross. In some instances, they have succeeded in deceiving true men, to the extent of obtaining introductions to respectable people, and the patronage of the government. They boast greatly of wonderful feats of bravery they performed during the late struggle: but it has generally fallen out, that whatever they did, under pretence of avenging their country's wrongs, was prompted by motives of private gain: and in no instance, has it failed to come to light, that they are mere wolves, in lion's skins, seeking under cover of that noble animal to prosecute their old trade, of plunder and of theft.

The universal staff officer, is represented in Brazil. And as many of them seemed to have little else to do, during the war, than to flirt with, and bring additional disrepute upon, that very small and insignificant class of women in the South (generally such as were born or educated in the North), who were easily smitten with the disease known as "button on the brain," they evince a disposition to continue their former employment here. But finding the flirting accessible in this city expensive, and realizing that the Confederate States are no longer in condition to maintain them in their unproductive speciality; they propose to marry some respectable lady, in order to obtain a support. They frequently dine, and drink with those, who are yet permitted to wear gay uniforms, and accompany these gentry to places of amusement and pleasure.

The attractiveness of tinselsy, and pocket change, accounts for their being together. And when we remember how little blood they have shed, in their own persons, we can understand the facility with which they take to each other, and speak of the past as forgiven and forgotten.

Lastly, in every sense, the New England fanatic, and propagandist, is represented in the dark land, which he intends to free, and enlighten, with his negro gospel. This representation consists chiefly, of so called missionaries and colporteurs, who distribute lying tracts, cant puritanism, and collect false statements for sensation book makers. They are, in many respects, the most pestilential class that can possibly infest any country.

[Note.—Chapter VIII. abridged from an elaborate article, by a Prussian gentleman of decided military ability, I print in this work, because our people are interested to know the defensibleness of the region chosen for their future homes.

From a careful examination of the whole country spoken of, with special reference to the subject herein treated, I arrived at the very same conclusions with the writer, long before I saw his article.

Cananeâ is the port at which we enter, in going to Iguape, our coast town: which is situated on Mar Pequeno, or little sea, forty-eight miles north of the point of entrance.

CHAPTER VIII.

CANANEÂ, PROVINCE OF SAN PAULO, AS A STRATEGIC POINT.

THE PORT OF CANANEA WITH THE RIVER REGION DOMINATED BY IT, IS, BY ITS STRATEGIC IMPORTANCE, THE KEY TO THE POLITICAL PREDOMINANCY OF THE SOUTH-BRAZILIAN PROVINCES, FROM SANTOS TO THE RIVER PLATE.

Brazil is protected in almost all its seacoast, against invasion from without, by the formidable Serra do Mar, only accessible with much cost, and in which a handful of men could crush an aggressive army, almost without wasting powder.

In this imposing fortress, nature, however, left a breach, which affords a commodious entrance into the interior, and gives easy access to the important depots of the State.

The Serra do Mar does not exist on the seacoast of the municipality of Cananeâ, whose depths are traversed by some outshoots of the Serra Negra, which starts from the Graciosa and runs with some interruptions almost to Iguape. It is from these interruptions that rivers come out, emptying their waters into those of the sea within Cananeâ, and *there* are the natural roads to the interior. Behind the serra commences immediately the fluvial region of the Ribeira de Iguape. This flows through an extensive basin, descending from the Serra Geral, at a distance of seventy-four miles approximately, through a gently falling terrene, so as to permit the descent of canoes from the top of the serra.

The terrene through which the principal tributaries of the Ribeira pass has exactly analogous conditions. This state of the formation of the terrene would at once allow the supposition of a facility for the establishment of communications, if this favorable circumstance were not already verified.

The port of Cananeâ is accessible for ships of great depth. The pilots affirm the bar to have seventeen feet four inches on it at low water. The bar is not difficult, and will not require pilots, when buoyed. The various arms of the sea, between the isles and the mainland, up to Iguape, afford a secure and extensive anchorage of 100 miles in length and 400 to 1,900 yards wide, with sufficient depth everywhere. The entrance of the bar, and its immediate continuations inwards are defensible in the most easy and efficacious manner possible, by simple beach batteries, made of the most proper material, sand, lined with fascines or wicker work. The isle of Bom Abrigo affords a safe anchorage outside the bar and still lies under the protection of the batteries. It is at the same time an excellent lookout point upon the sea.

I am then any power; I find it convenient, or am obliged to wage war against Brazil. I dispose of 20,000 soldiers, tolerably drilled and disciplined. I have just the number of ships of war and transports to conduct the army to its destination. I know the topography of the country better than the Brazilian government itself, because I find the port of Cananeâ at my disposal, undefended, and I find on land neither soldier nor organized militia to offer me resistance.

My little squadron enters the port without difficulty. I land my men, and the cannon destined for the batteries; and in a day the port is safe against any surprise by the enemy. At break of day the defensive works progress and can resist any regular attack. From this moment the fears cease, there is no need to suffer. There is excellent drinking water, fresh fish in abundance, and more than 20,000 producers are quite happy in delivering their produce to me. I have likewise a kind of Alabama which, from the isle of Bom Abrigo, looks out for the Brazilian merchant ships going to, or coming from the south, and she finds profitable occupation in boarding them and towing them into the port, and does not weary in continuing the same occupation.

I send a corps of 2,000 soldiers to Paranaguá, who within four days present themselves there without it being known whence they come; they go by land and rise suddenly, probably, at Guariquiçaba. They take possession of the war stores there existing, levy a moderate contribution, in which Antonina will take part, and they probably raze the fortress because I do not see that it can be of any use. Thenceforward nothing enters or goes out without my express license, and I will leave there only a small force as a corps of observation, which can communicate daily with Cananeâ.

A corps of 10,000 men is already placed in movement for the serra above, the vanguard of which arrive in eight or ten days' march, on the road that they will open, at Castro, in the Province of Paraná, intercepting every communication from the south, with the Province of São Paulo, and furnishing themselves in especial with horses, making raids as far as Curitiba on the other.

I left on purpose a corps of 8,000 at Cananeâ, to take charge of the fortifications and do the duties of their profession.

I fear everything from the mobility of the Brazilian forces forming in São Paulo, and I go to meet them, perhaps beyond Sorocaba, if for no other profitable object, to embarrass their march. I destroy the bridges in my return, and any other things that may offer. I am not, however, an enemy retiring from cowardice, I desire only to have my adversary in the convenient place, off Castro, and I begin my master movement. I order, two days before, a corps of 2,000 to open a road to the Capital of San Paulo, and within eight days I present a corps of 12,000 soldiers at the gates of that city, I intercept the railway and order the guarding of the serra road by a small force. Perhaps I make a visit to Santos. In any case the return of a corps, of those that went to attack me at Castro, and which may be sufficient to attack me, will be rendered difficult by the destruction of the bridges within a sufficient distance, which I ordered to be effected. Besides this, the road by which I came is exclusively mine and I can retire at the most proper moment, for I have no desire to sacrifice a single soldier uselessly. If my enemy wishes to fight me he will see himself rigorously necessitated to seek me at my head quarters at Cananeâ. He has even to come to me by land because he will not be able to force the port, or land any toops with the smallest success. He will come by the roads I opened, which he will find in good order because I have to use them to the last moment. My head quarters at Cananeâ has, however, only two entrances, made on purpose by nature, forming extended defiles which will be well furnished with batteries.

If the ammunition of the batteries last, the entrances will not be forced, and if the number of the enemy were infinite, their corpses will make the entrance almost impossible.

I say there are no grounds for admitting that my position may be taken, and my assailant will find it necessary to retreat, not thinking that I have already ordered him to be circled and his retreat made impossible.

After this victory I renew my incursions, to attract the enemy again. If he does not venture to attack me again at Cananeâ, he must at least protect the interior against my continual invasions, and employ for this a force at least four times superior to mine, on a line of defence of about 100 leagues, that is from San Paulo to Curitiba.

The Brazilian squadron (the enemy) may perhaps blockade the Port of Cananeâ, but at the same time must likewise blockade that of Paranaguá, if it is intended to do me any effective harm. Happily I have within the bounds of my power iron, lead, coal; as well as the ingredients of powder, or what may substitute it.

* * * * * * *

A road from the Port of Cananeâ to the Paraná is, in strategic and political points of view, of the highest convenience, if not of absolute necessity. It eclipses in importance and utility all the others that might be made to carry Brazilian power to the River Plate, and will be the shortest and least costly.

Considering this communication on its useful side, for the development of agriculture and commerce, a not less satisfactory result wil be found.

Starting from the port of Cananeâ, it crosses in a diagonal line the vast extent of public lands lying between the Ribeira and the Serra Negra, crossing the various rivers that flow to the Ribeira, and comes within a distance of ten leagues of the town of Bom Successo, above the serra which is upon the boundary of the Province. Thence it continues alternately through prairies and woods, scantily populated, and crosses the surveyed territories to the Colony of Assunguy, proceeding between settlements to Castro. With the navigation of the Tabagi, or any other serving better, the bottoms of these rivers would soon be animated with labor. The Province of Matto Grosso would find there its natural road. At a certain point of the road, six or seven leagues from Cananeâ, it is only five leagues from Iporanga, and therefore in contact with the settlements north of the Ribeira. And it is unquestionable that if this communication existed now, it would be along it that the American emigrants would establish themselves without hesitation, because there are no lands more suitable.

I conclude this succinct statement, observing that what I have said is not based on mere conjectures. Seven years I have studied this locality, partly in service of the Government, and in greater part for recreation. I crossed the backwoods of Assunguy and Cananeâ, on a right line between these two places; I have also explored that from San Paulo to the Ribeira, on the Juquiá. These two lines are the principal arteries for travel.

If I permit myself to point out the strategic importance of Cananeâ as eminent, it is merely with the authority of an old soldier of the Prussian Artillery.

THE GEOGRAPHICAL POSITION OF THE EMPIRE OF BRAZIL, AND THE BOUNDINGS OF THE SEVERAL PROVINCES WITHIN ITS LIMITS.

THE empire of Brazil lies between latitudes 4° 23′ north, and 32° 45′ south, and longitude 34° 56′ and 73° 20′ west from Greenwich; and is bounded north by Venezuela and the colonies of Guiana; northwest east and southeast by the Atlantic Ocean; south by Uruguay; southwest and west by the Argentine Confederation, Paraguay, Bolivia, Peru and Ecuador.

And contains 3,956,800 square miles; being over one-third larger than the United States. Its greatest diameter east and west, on the parallel of Cape Augustin (lat. 8.° 20′ s.) is 2,630 miles; and its greatest extent, north and south, on the medium of Cape Arange (long. 37° 27′ w.) is 2,540 miles; with a coast line 3,700 miles long.

PROVINCE OF AMAZONAS.

HOW BOUNDED.

This immense province stretches between 4° 23′ north latitude and 10° south latitude, and between 56° 59′ and 75° 3′ west longitude. It is bounded on the north by Guiana, Venezuela, and New Granada, being divided from these by the range of mountains which, under various names, runs along the northern boundary of Brazil; on the west by Equador and Peru, the Japurá, for part of its length, and the Javari, from south latitude 10°, forming most of the dividing line; on the south by Peru, Bolivia, and the province of Mato Grosso, the tenth degree of south latitude being the divisional line from the two first, and the rivers Madeira and Machado that from Mato Grosso.

Its length from east to west is 330 leagues, from north to south 280 leagues, and its estimated area 64,000 leagues.*

PROVINCE OF PARÁ.

HOW BOUNDED.

Pará, the most northern maritime province of Brazil, is bounded on the north-east by the Atlan-

* A Portuguese league equals four English miles.

tic, on the north by French Guiana; on the west by Amazonas, the river Neamunda forming, in part, the dividing line; on the south by Maranhão and Goyaz, the chief separating lines being made by the rivers Gurupy, Araguaya, Vertentes, Fresco, Atoary, Frez Barros, Tapajoz, and Oreguatus. It lies between 4° 15′ north latitude, and 9° 54′ south latitude, and 45° 54′ and 58° 59′ west longitude. Its superficial extent is estimated at 39,000 square leagues. Its capital is Belem or Pará, on the south side of the river Pará.

PROVINCE OF MARANHÃO.

HOW BOUNDED.

It is bounded on the north by the Atlantic, on the west by Pará, from which it is divided by the river Gurupy; on the south-west by Goyaz, the Tocantins and Manoel Alves Grande separating them; and on the south and east by Piauhy, the river Parnahiba being their boundary. Its length from north to south is 195 leagues, from east to west, 163 leagues; its seacoast, 130 leagues, and its area about 12,500 square leagues. It lies between 1° and 10° 45′ south latitude, and 40° 54′ and 49° 16′ west longitude.

PROVINCE OF SERGIPE.

HOW BOUNDED.

It lies between 10° 20′ and 1° 34′ south latitude, and 36° 11′ and 38° 25′ west longitude. It is bounded on the north by Alagôas, the river S. Francisco separating them; on the west and south-west by Bahia, the rivers Real and Hingo forming in part the boundaries; and on the east by the Atlantic. Its coast extent, from the Real to the S. Francisco is 30 leagues, from east to west 40 leagues, and its area about 1,200 square leagues. The capital is Aracajú.

PROVINCE OF PIAUHY.

HOW BOUNDED.

It lies between 2° 32′ and 11° 17′ south latitude, and 38° 38′ and 45° 59′ west longitude. It is bounded on the north by the Atlantic, on the west and north-west by Maranhão, from which the river Parnahiba separates it, on the south by Goyaz, the Serra dos Coroádos being the division: on the south-east, by Bahia and Pernambuco, and on the east by Cęará, the Serras dos Dois Irmãos, da Borborema and Ibiapaba forming their dividing boundaries. Its greatest length is from north to south-west 188 leagues, its breadth very unequal, and its area about 11,000 square leagues. It has only five leagues of sea-coast.

PROVINCE OF CEARÁ.

HOW BOUNDED.

It lies between 2° 35′ and 7° 9′ south latitude, and 36° 41′ and 40° 67′ west longitude. It is bounded on the north and north-east by the ocean, on the west by Piauhy, on the south by Pernambuco, and on the east by Parahyba and Rio Grande do Norte.

It has a sea-coast of upwards of 120 leagues and an area of 4,500 square leagues.

PROVINCE OF RIO GRANDE DO NORTE.

HOW BOUNDED.

It is bounded on the west by Ceará and Parahyba, from which the Serra of Apodi separates it; on the south by Parahyba; and on the north-east by the ocean. It has about 75 leagues of coast, and an area of 1,500 leagues. It lies between 4° 43′ and 6° 39′ south latitude, and 34° 53′ and 37° 24′ west longitude. Its capital is Natal.

PROVINCE OF GOYAZ.

HOW BOUNDED.

This province lies between 6° and 21° 40′ south latitude, and 44° 39′ and 53° 29′ west longitude from Greenwich. It is bounded on the north by Maranhão and Pará, the Manoel Alves Grande, the Tocantins, and the Araguaya separating them; on the west by Mato Grosso, the Araguaya and the Pardo being the dividing rivers; on the south by São Paulo and Minas Geraes, the Paraná and Parnahiba parting them: and on the east by Minas Geraes, Bahia and Piauhy, the line of division running along the Cordilhera, which has the various names along its range of Serra dos Crystaes, Chapada da St[a]. Maria, Serra da Tabatinga, and Serra das Coroadas.

It has a length of 300 leagues from the confluence of the Tocantins and Araguaya, to that of the Pardo and Paraná; an extreme breadth of 120 leagues, and a superfice of about 21,000 square leagues. Its capital is the city of Goyaz.

PROVINCE OF PARAHYBA.

HOW BOUNDED.

It lies between 6° 15′ and 7° 50′ south latitude, and 34° 36′ and 37° 52′ west longitude.

It is bounded on the north by Rio Grande, on the west by Ceará, on the south by Pernambuco, and on the east by the Atlantic ocean. It contains about 1,500 square leagues of surface.

PROVINCE OF PERNAMBUCO.

HOW BOUNDED.

This province is situated between the 6° 57′ and 11° 3′ south latitude, 34° 32′ and 41° 48′ west longitude.

It is bounded on the north by Parahyba and Ceará, from which it is separated by the rivers Abiahy and Popoco, and by the Serra das Imburanas; on the north-west by Piauhy, the Serra da Borborema being the boundary; on the south by Bahia and Alagôas, from which it is divided by the rivers S. Francisco, Casanova, and Persinunga; and on the east by the Atlantic. Its extension along its coast is 44 leagues; westward from Cape Agostinho to the Serra do Araripe 147 leagues, and its area about 6,000 square leagues.

ALAGOAS.

HOW BOUNDED.

This province lies between 8° 50′ and 10° 15′ south latitude and 35° 6′ and 37° 49′ west longitude. It is bounded on the north and west by Pernambuco, the dividing line being formed by the rivers Persinunga, Una, Jacuipy and Taquará, the Serra Pellada, and by the Moxoto, a tributary of the S. Francisco; on the south by the province of Sergipe, being separated therefrom by the S. Francisco, and on the east by the Atlantic. It has a seacoast extension of 56 leagues, and a superficies of 1,200 square leagues.

PROVINCE OF BAHIA.

HOW BOUNDED.

The province is situated between 9° 42′ and 18° 12′ south latitude, and 37° 9′ and 46° 9′ west longitude. It is bounded on the north by Sergipe and Pernambuco, being separated from the former by the river Real and from the latter by the S. Francisco, on the west by Minas, Geraes and Goyaz, the Serra dos Aimores dividing it from the first, and the Serra da Tabatinga and Chapada da St. Maria, from the last; on the south by Espirito Santo, the boundary being the Mucury, and on the east by the Atlantic ocean. Its extent from north to south is 160 leagues, from east to west 180 leagues, and its estimated area is 14,000 square leagues.

PROVINCE OF ESPIRITO SANTO.

HOW BOUNDED.

It lies between 17° 57′ and 21° 24′ south latitude, and 39° 17′ and 42° 7′ west longitude from Greenwich. It is bounded on the north by Bahia, the Mucury being the boundary; on the west by Minas Geraes, the Serras dos Aimorés, dos Arrepiados, and do Pico, and the river Preto dividing them; on the south by Rio Janeiro, the Itabapoana being the separating river; and on the east by the Atlantic. It has a seacoast of 90 leagues, an average width of 24 leagues, and a superficial area of 1,400 square leagues.

PROVINCE OF RIO DE JANEIRO.

HOW BOUNDED.

The territorial limits extend from 21° 35′ to 23° 25′ south latitude, and from 40° 58′ to 45° 7′ west longitude. It is bounded on the north by Espirito

Santo, from which it is separated by the river Itabapuana; on the north and north-west by Minas Geraes, separated therefrom by the rivers Preto and Parahyba and by the mountains of Mantigueira, on the south-west by the province of S. Paulo, and on the south and south-east by the Atlantic Ocean. The whole province contains about 2,400 square leagues.

The capital is Nitherohy, but its foreign port is Rio de Janeiro.

PROVINCE OF MATO GROSSO.

HOW BOUNDED.

This province lies between 7° and 24° south latitude, and 50° 4′ and 65° 29′ west longitude from Geenwich. It is bounded on the north by Pará and Amazonas, the separating rivers being Vertentes, Fresco, Aboary, Tres Barras, Tapajos, Oreguatus, Machado, and Madeira: on the west by Bolivia, the Madeira, Paragaú, Serra de Albuquerque, and Paraguay forming the principal bounding lines, on the south by Paraguay, the Appa, and the Serra do Maracujù being the frontier; and on the east by Paraná and Goyaz, the Paraná, Pardo, Pitombas, and Araguaya dividing the provinces. It has a length of 340 leagues, a breadth of 300 leagues, and a superficies of 51,000 square leagues.

The capital is the city of Cuiabá.

PROVINCE OF MINAS GERAES.

HOW BOUNDED.

It lies between 14° 30′ and 22° 32′ south latitude, and 39° 58′ and 52° 3′ west longitude. It is bounded on the north by Bahia, the chief limits being formed by the Serra do Garão Mogul, the Rio Verde Grande, and the Carunhanha; on the west by Goyaz, the Chapada da St[a]. Maria, the Serra dos Chrystaes, and the Parnahiba, dividing them; on the south by São Paulo and Rio de Janeiro, the Rio Grande Serra de Lopo, Serra da Mantiqueira, and the Parahyba, separating them; and on the east by Espirito Santo, the Serras dos Pico, dos Arrepiades, and Aimorés being the boundary. It is 150 leagues from north to south, and 220 from east to west, and has an area of 20,000 square leagues.

PROVINCE OF PARANA.

HOW BOUNDED.

It lies between 22° 18′ and 27° 33′ south latitude, and 47° 46′ and 54° 35′ west longitude. It is bounded on the north-east and north by São Paulo, the Itarére, and Paraná Panema separating them in great part; on the west by Mato Grosso, Paraguay and the Argentine Confederation, the Paraná Iguassú, S. Antonio, and Pipiryguassú dividing them; on the south-east by St[a]. Catharina, the Timbo, Serra do Mar, and Sahy, being the chief boundaries; and on the east by the ocean. It is 100 leagues long from north to south, 125 leagues from east to west, and has an area of about 6,000 square leagues.

Its capital is Curitiba, and its port and customhouse are at Paranaguá.

PROVINCE OF SAO PAULO.

HOW BOUNDED.

It lies between 20° and 25° 0′ south latitude, and 44° 18′ and 53° 23′ west longitude. It is bounded on the north by Minas, the Serra da Mantiqueira, Serra do Lopo, and the Rio Grande separating them on the west by Goyas and Mato Grosso, and Paraná dividing them; on the south by Paraná, the Paraná Panema and its tributary the Itarére forming the great part of the boundary; and on the south-east by the ocean. It is about 95 leagues from north to south, 170 from east to west, and has an area of about 11,000 square leagues.

The capital of the province is São Paulo, but its custom-house and port for foreign commerce are at Santos.

PROVINCE OF SÁO PEDRO DO SUL,

(otherwise)

RIO GRANDE DO SUL.

HOW BOUNDED.

This, the most southern province of the empire, is situated between 27° 12′ and 33° 43′ south latitude, and 49° 36′ and 57° 22′ west longitude. It is bounded on the south-east by the South Atlantic Ocean; on the north and north-east, by the rivers Pleotas and Mampituba; on the north-west by the Uruguay; and on the south by the Banda Oriental, the boundary line running along the Quarahy, the Serra de St[a]. Anna, the Jaguarão, and down the eastern shore of Lake Mirim, to the mouth of the little river Chuy, which empties into the ocean. From east to west, the length is 128 leagues, from north to south, 120 leagues, and its area is estimated at 9,000 square leagues, of which fully two-thirds is arable land.

PROVINCE OF ST[A]. CATHARINA.

HOW BOUNDED.

This province is situated between 25° 55′ and 29° 25′ south latitude, and 48° 43′ and 51° 41′ west longitude from Greenwich. It is bounded on the east by the ocean; on the north and north-west by Paraná, being separated therefrom by the river Sahy, by an offshoot of the Serra Geral, and by the river Timbo; and on the south-west by São Pedro do Sul, the rivers Pelotas and Mampituba forming the dividing line. The estimated area is 2,200 square leagues.

CHAPTER IX.

OFFICIAL REPORT NO. 1, OF REV. BALLARD S. DUNN, OF NEW ORLEANS, TO THE MINISTER OF AGRICULTURE ON THE VALLEYS OF THE ITAPEMIRIM AND ITABAPOANA, PROVINCES OF ESPIRITO SANTO AND RIO DE JANEIRO.

To His Excellency the Minister of Agriculture.

SIR: I have the honor to submit the following report:

On the 9th of November Commendador Carlos Pinto de Figueiredo met me at Rua da Alfandega, No. 31, and informed me that, in obedience to your order, he would be ready on the 11th to acoompany myself and companions on a tour of inspection and investigation, in the northern portion of the Province of Rio de Janeiro, and also in the southern portion of Espirito Santo. Accordingly, on the morning of the 11th we embarked on board the coast packet *Diligente*, in charge of Commendador Figueiredo, Mr. Henry Lewis acting in the capacity of interpreter for the expedition.

On the following day, at 4½ P. M., we reached the mouth of the pretty little river Itapemirim, where we went ashore, and were hospitably received and entertained for the night, by Sr. Antonio Ferreira Marques de Abreu. In the warehouse at this point we found considerable coffee, and some cotton; while on the beach we saw much rosewood and other valuable timber awaiting shipment. This, at the very threshold of our investigations, was an earnest for the fertility of the soil in the interior, as well as the wealth of the virgin forest.

This river is navigable at all times, for large canoes, to the first falls, some thirty miles from the mouth, and for small steamers a good portion of the year.

On the morning of the 13th, we ascended the river, in a kind of large yawl, to the village of Itapemirim, situated one and a half mile from the ocean. Here we met several Brazilian gentlemen of rank and culture, who received us very agreeably, and gave substantial proofs of the genuineness of their hospitality, by offering us every facility for prosecuting our journey, such as suitable animals, experienced guides, etc. At this point we remained two days, maturing our plans, examining maps, and getting all the little minutiæ ready for such an excursion.

While here I visited the sugar estate of Col. João Gomes, on the north side of the river, and was greatly surprised at the size and richness of the cane. Notwithstanding the near proximity of this plantation to the sea, the land should be classed as the best of its kind, and second, only, to the best character of soil.

It appears to be a coarse loam, in which decomposed granite, and decayed vegetation, from the mountains, around, and above on this river, are the principal ingredients.

This planter uses no other implement than the broad hoe. As I walked over these favorably situated lands, the thought kept pressing itself upon me, if they produce *such* cane under *such a system*, what would they yield under all the appliances of improved culture?

From this point we made an early start on the morning of the 15th, in a northerly direction, passing over a very rugged country, and at times very near the sea, until we reached the meagre little village of Orebo, situated on the Rio Novo, but a short distance from the coast, and about fifteen miles from Itapemirim. Here we breakfasted, and after resting a while, crossed the Rio Novo, and bore off westward up one of its branches, called Iconha.

After traversing a very fertile region, abounding

in mountains, beautiful cascades, rivulets, and springs, we reached the large coffee fazenda of Sr. Rodocanachi, known as Montebello. Here we were politely received, and entertained, by the proprietor and his accomplished lady, who made her appearance in the parlor and at table, suprising us very much by speaking English quite fluently.

This fazenda is beautifully situated, on the prancing, playful little river Iconha; now leaping over a precipice of several feet, now gliding away into the deep, dark foliage that overhangs its smiling face, as if to hide from observation, and now dividing, as if in a great hurry to see which half should beat the other round some little islet, that seemed for the moment the object of its coquettish attentions. I have never enjoyed any scenery more than that through which we passed from Orebo to Montebello. It burst upon us like a joyful surprise. The mountains that towered above on either side of the strèam, presenting a most inviting soil of a deep, dark vermilion hue, covered with gigantic trees of the useful and ornamental woods; while the ever varying parasites, that hang upon the trees, the vines, and the luxuriant undergrowth, made one almost feel and believe that the hands of sylphs have been about, festooning and rendering still more pleasing nature's exceedingly pleasing works. Add to all this, the sweet murmuring of many waters, enlivened by the witching notes of Brazil's own mocking birds; and whose ear so dull, or whose heart so heavy as not to respond to nature's rich and varied song?

From this fazenda we retraced our steps some ten miles, then took a southerly direction, until we reached the Rio Novo proper, where we bivouacked for the night, in the little colony known as Colony Rio Novo. For several miles before reaching this point, we traversed an extremely rough, yet fertile region. The lands belong chiefly to the Imperial Government, but much labor will have to be expended in making roads before it can be rendered available for culture. This part of the country is chiefly suitable for growing coffee. The next morning, the 17th, we continued our southerly course, until we reached the splendid coffee fazenda of Major Caetano, crossing mountains, rivulets, and everliving springs, in our journey to this hospitable gentleman's residence. Here we were received in true Brazilian style, refreshments for the body, and an intellectual feast for the mind, in the way of a running account of such things as we came here to learn. This gentleman's lands are of the best quality for coffee culture, and immense in quantity. There is a water power on his estate sufficient to propel a very great amount of machinery, and lumber enough, if properly sawn and used, to build a city. He showed us also a "gruta," or sort of cavern, in which his people, some forty in number, took shelter while opening the fazenda.

It is a remarkable opening, at the base of the mountain, in the large masses of granite that lie scattered around. To Major Caetano we are indebted for a choice troop of horses, on first setting out from Itapemirim, for which he has our sincere thanks. Having remained over night we repaired the next morning, the 18th, to Cachoeira, a distance of about seven miles.

Cachoeira is the new and thriving village at the head of navigation on the Itapemirim. Here we were warmly received by two young gentlemen engaged in the mercantile business at this point, who were friends, in their boyhood days, of our Commendador, in the Province of Minas. Their names are Monteiro da Gama and Carvalho; to these gentlemen we are indebted for much politeness and attention, which we hope some time to be able to return. This town, in my judgment, is destined, at no distant day, to become a place of some importance, situated as it is, at the head of navigation, and in the midst of a very large and fertile district of country. There is nothing lacking but an energetic population, who can, and will develop the resources of that region, to make it grow and flourish as a centre of trade. At Cachoeira we remained during Saturday, the 18th, and Sunday the 19th.

On Monday we visited the fazenda St[a]. Theresa, owned and conducted by Lieut. Col. Werneck, late of the Brazilian army. This splendid country seat is situated some twelve miles south of Cachoeira, and, as I suppose, midway between the rivers Itapemirim and Itabapoana. It is on a beautiful rivulet, surrounded by gigantic mountains, that stand like so many grim sentinels, keeping guard over the "sweet home" of refinement, and the fruitful fazenda that nestle at their feet. Col. Werneck is a gentleman of the olden school, and dispenses a magnificent hospitality, in the olden style; reminding me, almost painfully, of the palmy days of my own native Virginia, now gone, I fear, nevermore to return.

On the afternoon of the 22d, we returned to Cochoeira, and the next morning took up our line of march for the head waters of the Itapemirim; passing up on the south side until we reached a fazenda known as Duas Barras, where we halted and took dinner.

From Cachoeira to Duas Barras, some ten miles, the country is very beautiful and fertile, combining the richest water scenes, and the most peaceful looking valley landscapes, with towering mountains, on either side, spreading out to view very enticing coffee lands. Here we spent the afternoon and night very pleasantly, crossed the river just below the junction of two streams which form the Itapemirim, and continued on up the Rio Castello, on the north side, until we reached the fazenda Fructiera, situated on the north side of the Castello. From Duas Barras to this point, is about twelve miles, over a rugged, but extremely fertile country, nearly all of which is suitable for cultivation, particularly fitted for growing grapes and coffee.

At this fazenda we spent the night. The next morning, mounting early, we moved off rapidly over excellent soil, until we reached Fim do Mundo, a distance of about twelve miles.

This valuable estate is owned by a widowed daughter of the proprietor of Duas Barras. Here we took breakfast and spent the heat of the day, and after a long ride, of perhaps fifteen miles, reached the fazenda St. Quereno, owned and conducted by the very intelligent and scientific Dr. Antonio Olinto Pinto Coelho da Cunha. He is, also, an old friend of Commendador Figueiredo, from the Province of Minas. He was formerly engaged in mining for gold in that Province, but came to the conclusion, that the surest way to obtain a rich yield of the precious metal, was to bring his slaves down to the choice lands of Espirito Santo, and open a coffee fazenda. He did so, and is succeeding remarkably well. It is worthy of remark, too, that he employs little or no corporeal punishments among his slaves; believing that kind, firm treatment, giving them plenty to eat, is the surest way to get them to perform their duty in that state of life which it has pleased God to call them, and for which these child people were created. The Dr. seemed much amused at our fondness for sugar and cotton culture, and remarked: "A short residence in the country will cause you to transfer your affections to the great staple of Brazil." It is his decided opinion, that the culture of coffee is the most remunerative channel into which labor can be turned. In this I would be obliged to agree with him, if the *mode* of culture is to remain the same. That is, the mountain side shall continue to be scraped by no other implement than the broad hoe; while the level plains lie idle, or are only used as grazing grounds for the surplus stock of the plantation. But let these level lands be torn up by the fertilizing plow; let the numerous old logs and stumps that cumber the ground be removed, so that not a stalk nor a plant shall be missing, and these money yielding mountains will soon find competitors, in all that is useful, in the unpretending plains that now lie, unnoticed and uncared for, at their feet.

From this fazenda we moved forward, on the 25th, to Povoação, distant about four miles, on the head waters of Castello. This is another choice coffee fazenda in the midst of rugged mountains, and is the property of the hospitable Capt. Jose Vieira Machado; who gave us a most whole-souled welcome, and entered heartily into our views and wishes. In these comfortable quarters we remained two days, during which time it rained almost incessantly. While here we visited a very remarkable cavern, a brief description of which, I will here give; irrelevant though it may seem, in such a report as I am now making. It is situated one mile from the fazenda, and is entered by climbing up the side of a very steep mountain, about one thousand feet above the little valley that lies below. The entrance is an immense aperture in the side of the mountain, large enough for one hundred persons to stand, and look out upon the surrounding country, while they would be entirely sheltered by the huge cliff that projects at the cavern's mouth. After getting inside, it becomes irregular, and assumes the appearance of a vast suite of chambers, connected by numerous passages, some of them so low, that we were obliged to crawl, to get through. But once through, from one, into another, the grand and novel sight, of these stately vaulted halls, not made with hands, amply repays the toil of getting there. Many were the pleasant thoughts that soothed my mind, while traversing this subterranean abode of man and beast, in company with these remote descendants of the Latins; whose kindness and generous hospitality to me, a Christian Priest, beautifully contrasts with the fierceness of their fathers, of sixteen centuries ago, who drove the Christians of that age, to take refuge in caverns, similar to the one in which we then held pious converse, and mutually glorified the Great and Good God for the magnitude of his works. At one point we came upon an exceeding great shelf, or vault, which has at some remote time been the general cemetery of the aborigines of this country.

For there lie skeletons, grinning in their ghastliness, in great numbers, while the depth of dust upon their resting place, fully attests that the decree; "Dust thou art, and to dust thou shalt return," has been fulfilled upon thousands in this cavern. As I gazed upon this scene of death long past, I felt a desire to write, over these poor sons of the forest, that comforting saying of our Saviour, with which the burial service begins: "I am the resurrection and the life, saith the Lord; he that believeth in me, though he were dead, yet shall he live."

Captain Machado gave us much valuable information as to the manner in which those fazendas in that part of Espirito Santo were first opened. For, according to his account, in that portion of the province of Minas, from which they nearly all came, about fourteen years ago, they began to feel themselves crowded; and when they began to look around for lands upon which to settle their children, they found such lands were not to be had. So a considerable number of them, who were of the same way of thinking, agreed that they would remove into the province of Espirito Santo.

Upon reaching the fine coffee lands were they now live, in such luxury, they all went to work, and opened one common fazenda, to which they gave the name of Centro. Here they built and planted; and, from this common centre, in a few years have grown some of the most desirable fazendas in the Province.

From Povoação, on the morning of the 29th, with Captain Machado at the head of the column, we were up and away for Centro; the original head quarters, of which he had spoken so much. On reaching this mangnificent fazenda, we were very kindly received, by the proprietor Major Machado da Cunha, who is a quiet dignified gentleman, well advanced in years.

Here, as at all our stopping places, we were made to feel ourselves entirely at home. We had been but a short time under the tiles when the rain sat in afresh. On reaching Major da Cunha's, we learned that it would be impossible to traverse, or even penetrate, the large tract of government land that lies on the head waters of the Grandú, a tributary of the Rio Doce. This was a grievous disappointment, as we had every reason to believe that there is a very desirable tract of land in that locality. But the obstacle that here presented itself was such as our brief time would not permit us to overcome. The time and labor requisite to open roads, or even paths such as we would gladly have crept through, to see these lands, placed the matter beyond our control.

After collecting all the information attainable on the subject, my conclusion is, that what we would have seen on the Grandú, would have been almost a repetition of what we had seen and examined on the head waters of the Itapemirim.

At Centro we remained two days, and were very agreeably entertained by the hospitable inmates of the spacious mansion, which has arisen upon the site of the wigwams of fourteen years ago. After a free consultation on the morning of the 29th, we deemed it best to retrace our steps to Duas Barras, on the Itapemirim, which point we reached on the 30th, where our reception and entertainment on our return was of like character with that which we received as we passed up.

Remaining at Duas Barras over night, we pursued our journey up the south side of the main branch of the Itapemirim, on the morning of December the 1st, reaching Bananal, a distance of seven miles, where we took breakfast. The lands from Duas Barras to Bananal are very desirable.

They are equally fertile with those on the northern branches of the same river, while their position is more favorable for improved culture.

The mountains are less rugged, the hills more gentle and rounded, the streams quite as frequent, and the valleys larger. Altogether the change is a pleasing one. This proprietor has a fine water power, and a very creditable mill in operation.

Having finished breakfast, we continued our journey up the river until we reached fazenda Bartholomeu, where we remained over night.

The next morning, December 2d, after a delightful ride of three miles, over lands that are perfectly lovely, we stopped to breakfast at one of the most highly improved fazendas in all that part of the country. It is known as Felicio de Lacerdo. The young man who received us, showed himself a gentleman, both in instinct and culture. On this estate we met with the first herd of cattle that we had seen during the journey. Every planter has a few head, but not enough to be called a herd. This gentleman has near two hundred head, many of them the improved breeds from Europe. We moved forward, the next morning, December 3d, after a most agreeable entertainment, to the village of Alegre, where we halted and obtained a guide to conduct us on our journey; which now lay through a region not much traversed. Alegre is a cleanly looking little place, situated very prettily on some small hills in the midst of very fertile lands.

After resting an hour or two, taking coffee, mounting our new guide, &c., we were off again, up and down, over the mountains and some very rugged country, until we reached a pretty little fazenda called Café. Here we spent the night; took an early start the next morning, wound our way through some of the very best lands we had yet seen, and, at about 3 o'clock, brought up at the appropriately named fazenda Cachoeira Bonita. At this point we found the proprietor, José Francisco Furtado, a very intelligent man, building a new house of large dimensions, into the finished portion of which he received us cordially. After a thorough examination, we came to the conclusion that, *naturally*, his is the most beautiful situation we had ever seen. The mountains on either side, slope gently down, terminating in a beautiful valley between them. In the midst of this valley, there is a mound, or island, about fifty feet high, containing near five acres, as graceful and equal all round, as if thrown up, and shapen by the hand of man. The little rivulet Cacado, upon which the fazenda is situated, as it flows against the island, divides, and, flowing equally round, the halves rejoin each other, moving joyously through the verdant foliage and fragrant flowers in the peaceful vale below; reminding one of a wedding scene, where two loving souls are united in holy wedlock's bonds, and set out afresh on life's hopeful voyage.

Leaving a region where nature has bestowed such abundant charms, the next morning, December 5th, we soon reached the little village São João Cacado; where we halted for a short time to make some enquiries about roads, animals, etc. Pushing forward through rain and mud, we reached a very extensive establishment, which, if we judge by the amount of land once in cultivation, has been at one time an important fazenda. But now everything bears evident signs of decay. The aged widow of the former proprietor, received us very kindly, and did everything in her power to make us comfortable. The country through which we passed, on our way to this fazenda, from Cachoeira Bonita, most of which is in a state of nature; is truly rich, truly beautiful. Breakfasting with our worthy hostess, on the morning of December 6th, we mounted, and after a ride of seven miles, reached the ferry on the Itabapoana, at the village of Bom Jesú.

At Bom Jesú, we were very much delighted at a little exhibition of good feeling, on the part of the citizens, towards our excellent friend, Commendador Figueiredo. We had no sooner put foot on the south side of the river, than up went a shower of rockets; followed by other and larger reports, which continued until we reached our hotel. His modesty on the occasion was truly refreshing. As we walked across the square, amid the rapid reports of bursting rockets, he turned to me, and remarked in very good English, most of which he has learned on this journey: 'The people are content to see the Americans come.' Thus giving to others, the honors intended for himself. We soon discovered that he is looked upon by the inhabitants on this river, as a public benefactor, and treated with marked respect on all occasions. His successful efforts in opening this valuable river to steam navigation, have justly endeared him to the people.

At Bom Jesú, we remained five days, during which time Commendador Figueiredo visited his aged father, some fifteen miles higher up the river. This village is small and insignificant at present, but situated in the midst of lands which if occupied and cultivated, would soon develop it into a prosperous inland town. During our stay here, we were the guests of Sr. Carlos Rociques Firmo, a brother in law of our Commendador.

He and his truly estimable lady entertained the party very pleasantly. I have rarely seen any one of so much excellence, and yet, withal, so unobtrusive as this lady. From here we made a start, on the 11th of December, down the Itabapoana, reaching Fortaleza, a large and flourishing fazenda, owned by José Carlos de Campos, who gave us comfortable quarters for the night.

The proprietor has a large and excellent tract of land, nearly all of which is susceptible of improved culture.

On the morning of the 12th we resumed our journey coastwise, reaching, late that afternoon, the fazenda São Pedro, one mile above the head of navigation on the Itabapoana, at the mouth of a little river bearing the same name. At this point we found much the largest and most expensive residence I have seen in the interior, in process of erection. The main building is 40 by 80 feet, with wings running back 70 feet; intended to enclose a large court for flowers, etc. The 80 feet front, overlooks the river, which, for more than a mile, forms, together with the verdant valley through which it winds, all closed in by the lofty mountains covered with immense trees and every species of parasite, a landscape of unusual attractiveness.

Early on the morning of December 13th, we mounted and rode down to Limeira, a little village situated at the head of navigation on the Itabapoana.

Breakfasting here, we got ready to embark on board the little steamer *Itabapoana*, which was to bear us hence to the ocean. In looking about this village, and making inquiry, I found that the amount of coffee here shipped for Rio de Janeiro, or rather to the mouth of the river there to be transhipped, was very considerable. The question occurred to me, while making these investigations, if the commerce of this little river has already reached this magnitude, with the present sparse and unsystematic population; what will it be, when thoroughly occupied by a population who use all the appliances of improved culture?

At 3 o'clock, we went on board, and steamed down the river some five miles, when we stopped and put up for the night, at Sr. A. Guera's splendid fazenda. Here we met with every attention, on the part of the proprietor, who made us feel altogether at home.

The lands from Limeira to within ten miles of the coast, a distance of thirty miles, are of the best quality. Their *position* is far more desirable than any I had seen up to that time.

The valleys are wider, varying from one to three miles, and terminating in gentle acclivities, all of which seem to invite the husbandman to a fruitful home, and these in turn losing themselves in the stately and graceful mountains, that rise up between the Itapemirim and the Itabapoana, on the north, and the Itabapoana and the Parahyba, on the south. As I gazed upon this magnificent prospect, and felt my heart warm with real delight in the contemplation; and at the thought of new homes for old loves, I imagine my feelings, in contrasting the valley of the Itabapoana, with that of the more rugged, yet very fertile Itapemirim, were somewhat similar to what we may suppose would be those of a great admirer of female beauty; who should gaze upon the charms of a mountain maiden, famed for her beauty, yet with a somewhat stately and severe aspect, with features inclining to the aquiline; and then, as she moves majestically away, cast his eyes upon another of Grecian mould, with the exquisite graces of refinement and ennobling culture superadded.

On the morning of the 14th, we went on board the little steamer, that lay chafing at the landing, as if impatient to have us come, and then gliding pleasantly down the placid little Itabapoana, reached the village at its mouth, bearing the same name, at 3 o'clock P. M. This day's travel was through the centre of what is known as the Jesuit tract; which was the first body of land large enough, and level enough, for homes for those for whom I pioneer. If the Imperial Government of Brazil, could see its way clear, to introduce our people into this portion of the Empire, under circumstances favorable to those whose aching hearts have been riven by the dread horrors of war; I humbly believe that the benefit would be mutual within a few years. The same broad acres, which now lie idle, producing nothing of profit, would become a fruitful source of revenue; and, at the same time, the happy home of a brave, honorable, peace loving people. Here we could relate the story of our disasters to our children, and teach them, that a government to be *just* and *equitable*, must be *permanent* and *stable;* and not the creature of caprice, to be changed by every popular gust of passion. This tract, however, has an objection, which is this: it is too accessible to an invading force from the coast, in case of war. This will seem to the peaceful Brazilians, a remote contingency, against which to be guarding. So it would have *seemed* to us, five years *ago.* But sad experience has taught us, that great advantages, in the way of accessibility, carry with them *dangers* of corresponding magnitude. If I were permitted to choose between this tract, and another of equal value, more remote from the operations of gunboats, I would certainly prefer the safe locality.

At the mouth of this river, as also at the head of navigation, in the capacious warehouses of the Navigation Company, we found much produce waiting shipment. Here, too, we saw much rosewood and valuable ship timber in process of preparation for shipment.

On the morning of the 15th, we mounted choice saddle horses, furnished by the polite, and accommodating Major Edward de Oliveira, and bore off southward, along the coast to S. João's bar, at the mouth of the Parahyba, a distance of twenty-five miles. Twenty miles of this journey was made on horse-back, the remaining five in a large canoe, down one of the lagoons that empty into the Parahyba, at the Barra de S. João. Finding here, that we could not return to the capital before the 20th, our energetic Commendador resolved to shew us the good city of Campos, and the valley below.

The town of Barra de S. João, contains a population of about four thousand. But the place bears evident signs of decay. This the inhabitants ascribe to the more rapid growth, and greater prosperity of Campos, forty-five miles up the river. Why the growth of an interior city should impede the prosperity of one on the coast, with the advantage of being favorably situated for light draught ship building; and, at the same time, the entrepot through which all commerce is obliged to pass, I could not understand. Here we found two new schooners on the stocks, and several old ones undergoing repairs. There was also much ship timber at the bar.

On the afternooon of the 16th, we went on board the little river packet *Agente*, and steamed away for Campos. We had not gone far when the extreme loveliness of the landscapes, as we glided through them, caught the attention of the whole party. The placid, gently flowing Parahyba, with its many enchanting islands, clothed in perpetual verdure, resembling so many emerald stones, in one vast setting of silver; with fazenda after fazenda, abounding in the most luxuriant growth of everything that a fertile soil, a salubrious climate, and an eternal summer can produce; spreading out their vast extent to the admiring gaze of the delighted voyager, and the whole girt about with the mellow chain of mountains beyond, with occasionally a lofty peak, rearing its towering head, as if to pierce the very heavens; all conspire to form, as it were, a panoramic view of rare and exceeding beauty.

While in Campos, we visited the fine sugar estate of Commendador Julião Ribeiro Castéo, a very public spirited gentleman, one mile from the city. This plantation is finely situated, and the most advanced in the mode of culture that I have seen while on this tour. It was here that we met with the first plow. His sugar house, distillery, &c., are very creditable to the establishment.

On the 19th, we returned on the steamer *Agente*, to Barra de S. João; where we went on board the coast-packet *Ceres*, only to find, at the moment of starting, that the boat had too much cargo to cross the bar, and that we would have to lie over twenty-four hours for the rising of the tide. On the 20th, at a ¼ to 4, we steamed out of the harbor, and had a delightful run, of about twenty hours, to the Capital.

Very respectfully,
Your obedient Servant,
BALLARD S. DUNN.

CHAPTER X.

OFFICIAL REPORT NO. 2. OF REV. BALLARD S. DUNN, OF NEW ORLEANS, TO THE MINISTER OF AGRICULTURE, ON A PORTION OF THE PROVINCE OF SAN PAULO.

ILLUSTRIOUS SIR: I have the honor to submit the following report of my second tour of observation. On the 9th of January, I embarked on board the coast-packet, "D. Affonso," supposing we should leave at 3 P. M., as advertised; but from some cause we did not go until the next day at 9 A. M. After a most unpoetical voyage, in a slow, and comfortless steamer, we reached Cananeâ on the afternoon of the 13th at 5 P. M. Here I found Sr. Ernesto D. Street, Inspector General of Public Lands; who promptly forwarded your Excellency's orders to Director Smith, at his residence, twelve miles interior, in the Colony of Cananeâ, who as promptly obeyed; reporting at my lodgings, early on the morning of the 15th, with the gratifying intelligence that he was ready, with good animals, to conduct me to the colony, and farther, when desired.

Duing the two days that I remained in the village of Cananeâ, I obtained some very curious information. I believe it is not generally known, that this, next to St. Vincent's, some distance north on the coast, is the oldest European settlement in the Western Hemisphere. It is matter of record, that the Portuguese landed here in 1535, and at that early date gave to the island the name of Cananeâ, or Canaan. The church here is very ancient, being now in its two hundred and sixty-fifth year. The island of Cananeâ is about sixteen miles long by five miles wide. It has one mountain, several springs of excellent water, and the soil in places produces well under a poor system of culture. The harbor is excellent, but the village is insignificant, and in a very delapidated condition. The inhabitants subsist chiefly on fish and rice, with a little fat pork and dried beef.

On the 15th I repaired to the Colony of Cananeâ in company with Director Smith. Our road thither was, most of the way, through the lands of the colony. After getting some four miles from the coast, the distance which the poor lands of the sea-shore here extend, we began to pass through a more fertile region. The colonial road, a short distance from the coast, crosses the little river Itapetanga, which flows though the colony from west to east. This road is up the main branch of the Itapetanga to its source; thence across the mountain, which divides the waters of the Pindavina—a tributary of the Garahú, from those of the Itapetanga, and on down the rivulet Pindavina, to the western extremity of the colony.

It is in places a tolerable road, for pack mules; and in other places might be very much improved by a little labor judiciously expended; but a large portion of it will require much labor, and some good engineering, to render it passable for wagons and carriages. As I traversed this colony in various directions, in company with the Director, and spoke of its susceptibility of improvement, his reply was: "A general can do nothing without soldiers." The application, to my mind, was obvious. He is there with a few superannuated men, most of them verging towards three score years, who are poor in the extreme; who, if ever they had any aspirations after a better estate, have lost them entirely. This reminds me, that I have found, by observation, in South America, as in North America, that vicious Europeans, are not improved morally, intellectually, nor industrially by emigration. On the contrary, they easily fall into the indolent habits of the more virtuous and ingenuous natives of the lower classes. The fruitfulness of Brazil is such, that they can subsist almost without exertion; therefore they cease to perform that labor, which necessity, in their native land, rendered compulsory.

The soil throughout this colony, is very peculiar. In places it has the compact, adhesive quality of the best vermilion-colored earth, but of a greyish, ashy color. It appears to rest upon a uniform bed of yellowish clay. Loose boulders are to be found of detached pieces of granite; also a hard, flinty gravel appears in places on the surface. I noticed, too, in many places, a soft kind of quartz, resembling very much a soiled mass of alum.

On the 17th Inspector-General Street detailed Sr. Manoel Cunha Sampaio, an engineer of the commission, and a Brazilian gentleman of education and refinement, to accompany me farther into the interior, in the capacity of engineer and interpreter. Accordingly, on the morning of the 18th, Sr. Sampaio joined me in the colony, and we sat out for the Colony of Pariquera, passing up the Itapetanga, crossing the mountain, which separates its waters from those of the Garahú, and down the rivulet Pindavina, to where it falls into the Garahú. Here we stopped to breakfast, at Mr. Francisco Cavier's, after a morning-ride of twelve miles. Breakfast despatched, we took a canoe, and descended the Garahú to its confluence with the Jacupiranga—a distance of six miles, then on down the Jacupiranga to Botujurú—a kind of trading post and fazenda, where we put up for the night. The lands of the Garahú and Jacupiranga are very fertile: better suited, however, for the culture of sugar cane and tobacco, than for the staple products of the country. The river bottoms are generally very level, and somewhat subject to overflow; but I believe these overflows to be of such short duration as not to prove detrimental to the growing crops. At any rate, I noticed a fine field of corn, through which the water passed to the depth of two feet several days before, which seemed to have sustained no injury, but rather to have been invigorated by the irrigation.

On the morning of the 19th, we resumed our voyage down the Jacupiranga, reaching Hildebrande, a fazenda on the river, at 9 P. M., where we spent the night. At this point my suspicions that these lower river lands are subject to a sort of low, malarious fever, were confirmed. I examined a boy here, who suffers from what the physicians term "enlargement of the spleen," but better known throughout the miasmatic districts of the United States, to the common people, as "ague-cake." That many of their trifling ailments, and much of the tallow-facedness that we see, are due to their habits, and the meagre diet upon which they subsist, there can be no doubt.

On the morning of the 20th, we were again in our canoe, darting swiftly down the Jacupiranga, which soon carried us out on the broad, blue face of the deep, majestic Ribeira. Down the Ribeira we glided smoothly, reaching the town of Iguape at 9 P. M. Iguape is beautifully situated on an island, formed by Mar Pequeno, or Little Sea, the river Ribeira, and an artificial canal, which connects the river with Mar Pequeno. If we were to judge by the immense fleet of canoes that line this splendid beach, and the numerous stores, and shops that are open, the commerce of Iguape is by no means insignificant; but, upon close examination I have found it very trifling. While here, I went up on the Mount of View, an elevation of some two thousand feet above the level of the sea, and there I found that it had been appropriately named; for the view is one of the grandest I have yet enjoyed in this land of the magnificent and sublime. The mountain is situated near the centre of the island. From its summit I could see the placid Mar Pequeno, stretching out fifty miles, separating from the mainland Ilha do Mar, or Island of the Sea—varying in width from one to two miles—covered all over with everliving green—lying amiably, but firmly there—opposing a quiet yet effective barrier to the farther progress of the mighty Atlantic—forming part of a picture over which the Christian's eye will ever wander with almost inexpressible delight. But when I extended my gaze beyond the island, far out upon the broad expanse, which now spreads out for many dreary thousands of miles, between this land of hope, and that which gave me birth, I could not repress the heart swelling, as I thought of the dear ones beyond where those dark, blue waters roll. Turning a little, I could look down on the busy town of Iguape, which lies snugly in at the foot of the mountain. Everything below wore the appearance of a gala-day. Bell-ringing, drums, sky-rockets, banners, and processions were the order of the day: for that was the feast of St. Sebastian. Turning still farther, my eyes rested upon the blue mountains of peaceful Brazil, far away interior, where many a silver rivulet sweetly winds between, and many a lovely valley spreads out its soul-inspiring landscapes, inviting to a land of comfort, my own distressed countrymen, thousands of whom, I humbly trust, will at no very distant day, there bivouac, and learn to call it home.

On the afternoon of the 20th we had everything ready for an early start the next morning, when very unexpectedly Dr. Gaston, of South Carolina, arrived from Xiririca, and being engaged in a similar work, we thought it best I should defer leaving one day, that we might compare notes, and each get the benefit of the other's experience. Most of the 21st was so occupied. Dr. Gaston is a highly cultivated, candid, sensible man, and his notes evince the fact that he is an accurate observer.

On the 22d we left Iguape, and toiled up the Ribeira to the mouth of the little river Pariquera, where we arrived late in the evening, and stopped for the night. On the morning of the 24th, we commenced the ascent of the Pariquera, which we found a crooked, muddy little stream, deep enough for navigation when swollen as at that time, but too shallow for anything but small canoes when low, according to the account of those who reside upon its banks. Late in the afternoon we reached a bluff on the river, and made our arrangements to spend the night. This bluff is owned and occupied by an old mulatto man, who has a large family of little children, and who treated us very kindly. We hired him to accompany us the next day, to the Colony of Pariquera, where we arrived at 3 o'clock, P. M. on the 25th. Dr. Sampaio and myself got out of the canoe at the lower line of the colony and walked across its lands to the nucleus—some six miles, the better to judge of the character of the soil. The lands of this colony are similar to those of Cananeâ, but inferior in quality. The buildings put up by the government are very large and commodious. There are three, all of the same dimensions—about seventy-five by thirty-five feet, and in a good state of preservation. Should emigrants elect to go there, they will find ample shelter for a large number. As for myself, I am convinced that neither the locality, nor the quality of the soil would suit our people. There are already some thirty families of squatters on these lands.

It was here I saw a great curiosity in the way of a plow. It is very large, very clumsy, and as nearly as I can judge, after the pattern in use in Europe two centuries ago. This plow has a cast plate nailed to the beam, marked, "Paris." I should be sorry to have Brazilians judge of the utility of plows, by a trial of this one. On the morning of the 26th we commenced the descent of the Pariquera, reaching a fazenda bearing the name of Vincent's, late in the afternoon. Here we remained over night. Vincent's is the most desirable locality I saw on the Pariquera River. It is owned by Mrs. Maria Gonçalves de Mangunca, a widow lady, who treated us very hospitably.

Leaving this point early on the morning of the 27th, we reached the mouth of the river, in time to ascend the Ribeira one league, where we got lodgings for the night with a colored man, who owns several thousand acres of valuable land, but subsists chiefly upon fish, taken from the Ribeira, and rice raised upon a small field not yet enclosed. Up the Ribeira we toiled all day of the 28th, reaching Ponta Grossa late at night. The 29th was spent at Ponta Grossa, examining this magnificent estate; magnificent, I mean, in its undeveloped resources. First, I inspected a field of cotton on the south side of the river, containing, I suppose, about eighty acres. This cotton is from imported North American seed, is now about five months old, and, as a general thing, about five feet high. It is well filled with blooms and bolls, some of the latter beginning now to open.

I am sorry to be obliged to note almost a fatal mistake in the planting and management of this cotton. In North America it would prove entirely fatal. First of all, the ground is new. Having been cleared, or rather chopped and burnt off, just previous to planting. No plow has yet been used, either in preparing the soil or cultivating the cotton. But the slaves have taken the cotton seed, just as the North American Indians take corn, and after opening a small orifice in the virgin soil, placed the seed carefully in, and then raked a little soil upon it. When the young plants were up, and the weeds began to grow, they went in with broad hoes, and, scraping *from* the plant, cleared away the weeds. Here the culture has ended: so that the cotton stands in the middle of a considerable *depression*, instead of upon an elevation of eight or ten inches above the general level, as its health and maturity require.

As a consequence, I noticed that the lower bolls, which are entirely excluded from a free circulation of the air, are inclined to rot and fall off. This would not have happened if the sun and air had been permitted to do their work in crisping and drying the ripening bolls. While traversing this field, the overseer, who had me in charge, pulled up a single plant of the ground pea, alias "Guber," and, to my astonishment, it brought up a full pint of the very best developed and matured peas I ever saw.

Oh! thought I, if the North Carolinians, and

Georgians, could but see that cluster, how they would make haste to dispose of their piney woods fields and bald clay knobs, that they might emigrate to Brazil. From this field we crossed the river to another of much larger dimensions—perhaps two hundred acres, which was also cleared last year, and is what we should term *up-land.* That is, upon an undulating table land, about one hundred feet above the level of the river. The soil is entirely different from that of the river bottom. From here to the mouth of the Pariquera, which empties into the Ribeira some twenty miles from the sea coast, the bottoms are a rich loamy earth, resembling very much the soil on the Mississippi and its tributaries. The table lands on the lower Ribeira, are not so good as these rich bottoms; yet they are of good quality. The character of the soil is that of a coarse, dark sand, very heavily surcharged with the fine fertile matter of decayed vegetation, and very friendly to cultivate. As a general thing the soil is not deep, but rests upon masses of compact clay, which will make it wear well. This large field is also planted in herbaceous cotton. The young plants are now some two months old and about knee-high. They have a healthy color and seem to be growing well; but the same lack of a practical knowledge of planting is here apparent, which I have described, on the other side of the river.

From Ponta Grossa we started, at peep of day, on the morning of the 30th, and at 9 A. M. stopped to breakfast at Sr. David Gonçalves Fortes'. Here a day was lost in waiting for a Brazilian gentleman, who had engaged to accompany us up the Juquiá River. Finding that he was not coming, we got Sr. José Rodolpho Gonçalves Fortes, a brother of our host, to act as pilot and guide, and started for the Juquiá. We had gone some ten miles up this river, when night overtook us, just as we were nearing a very small establishment, where we obtained shelter for the night. At gray dawn we were off again, forcing our immense canoe to stem the deep, swift current of the bold Juquiá. This was a day of toil, and when it was over, just as the glorious day-god was sinking out of sight behind the grand old range of mountains, that lay off to the westward of us, we reached the romantic little village of Santo Antonio, where we were received, and hospitably entertained, by the Rev. Rector, of the neat little church, which stands upon one of the beautiful mounds that here approach very near the river. Again, early on the morning of the 2d, we might have been seen urging our great river horse, with pole and paddle, to ascend still farther the deep, flowing river. This day's journey was to me like the realization of a fond dream of happiness. At every turn of the beautiful stream I felt like exclaiming, "Eureka! Eureka!" The magnificent valley of the Juquiá, which is very wide in places, terminates in a gentle range of hills, every foot of which, both hills and valley, are susceptible of improved culture. Back of these hills rise up great fertile mountains, that seem to have laid aside the nodding crest of threatening granite, and to be paternally contemplating the hills below, and the river that rolls between, or offering friendly salutations across from one to another, as if conscious of the mighty dignity in which they there repose. I have had bright day dreams, for many months, of a country where the homes of the great staple products of the world could be found in close proximity.

And here it is. If four brothers, or friends, wish to engage in the culture of the four great commercial products of Christendom, and have their plantations adjoining each other, they can here do so. They who wish to cultivate cotton and sugar cane, can find a most genial and productive soil immediately on the river. The tobacco raiser and the coffee planter, need not go out of sight to find the mother land of the coffee tree and the tobacco plant, on the gentle hills, or the giant mountain side. And each may raise upon his own plantation all the minor products, yea, all the luxuries of this luxury producing country. The crowning glory of Juquiá country is this: while it combines all characters of fertile soil, each is the best of its kind. The mountains are fully equal, if not superior, to those of Espirito Santo, and Rio de Janeiro, for the growth of coffee, while the hills and valleys surpass any part of the country I have seen for sugar, cotton, and rice. As proof of the correctness of my statements, I will here give the dimensions of a coffee tree, which I measured at Sr. José Dionisio Sanches', on the north bank of the Juquiá. This tree is twenty-eight inches in circumference, one foot from the ground, is fifteen feet high, and around its greatest circumference of foliage is sixty-eight feet. I ought to state that there is a slender young tree standing very near the trunk of the large one, whose foliage was included in this measurement. This tree, however, might be removed, and not diminish the outline of the one measured, so completely is it encircled by the boughs of the great one. From the two, the proprietor informed us, he gathered forty-two pounds of coffee last year. This young giant is now in his eighth year.

Late in the afternoon of the 2d, we arrived at the plantation of Sr. José Rodolpho Gonçalves Fortes, where we went ashore, and, after looking round a little, were so much delighted with the country, that we thought it expedient to penetrate somewhat the interior. Accordingly, everything was arranged for an early start next morning. Immediately after breakfast, Dr. Sampaio, myself, an old Brazilian hunter as guide, and two servants, commenced a pedestrian march up the beautiful rivulet that flows through this plantation, to which, finding it nameless, I gave the name of Brook Cornelia, after my first-born. Just as we were ready to start, our guide informed us that there was a high waterfall on this brook, which we could reach by going right forward before night. At the thought of a roaring cascade, in the deep, dark, forest, surrounded by cool dripping springs, my heart fairly bounded forward in enthusiasm. Away we went, the old guide in front, armed with his long wood's knife, with which he slew alike, the tender, blooming reed, and the tough, hardy vine, that ventured to extend themselves across our path; while I followed close upon his heels, urging him to take longer strides and bolder strokes; Dr. Sampaio and the two blacks bringing up the rear. In this order we marched, with many a break in the ranks, to get water, pluck fruit, or examine curious things, until about 3 P. M., when a dark cloud made its appearance in the south-west, and distant thunder could be heard. At this our guide shook his head, gave an ominous shrug of his shoulders, and advised that we go no further, but stop, make ranche, and so get ready for the threatening storm. To this, however, I would not agree; but suggested to Dr. Sampaio, that he and the servants stop and extemporize a camp, while the guide and I would go forward to the fall, and return, if possible. To this the Dr. readily consented. When it was fully decided that the line of march should again be taken up, though with ranks very much thinned, the old hunter informed me that we should save time by going right up the channel of the stream. Anything, said I, to reach the fall, and get back before night. So in we went, and off we started, at a rapid pace for waders. We had not gone far, when we came upon the fresh tracks of an anta, and as one deep hole in the wet sand (where his immense weight had forced his huge feet), after another, greeted our eyes, the old woodsman seemed to grasp his long knife more firmly, while I kept my revolver in a position for instantaneous use. But we never came up with him, consequently we did not get to kill an anta. After some two miles of wading in water as pure, cool, and clear, as any I ever saw, we reached the fall. And although a few moments of inactivity served to convince me that my muscles were rendered sore, and my joints stiffened like those of an overstrained courser, I felt compensated for all, by the rapturous beauty of the scene. This cascade leaps, at one bound, from the top of a perpendicular rock, sixty feet high, and strikes with such force upon the rocky bed below, that the whole volume is knocked, instantaneously, into spray. But the fragments soon collect again, and go laughing and dancing over many small falls below, until the re-united springs and sprays, form again one beautiful stream, which soon reaches a point where it behaves with more dignity and composure. The deepening shadows, of the shady dell, warned us that it was time to commence retracing our steps to the spot where we expected to spend the night. Slowly, and with pain to my physical system, did I return to that new-made wigwam in the depths of the virgin forest. But the rich glow of hope that then animated my bosom, and the bright gleams of anticipation which I then felt, seemed to illuminate my whole being. After returning to camp, and drying my clothes as best I could, I was too weary to sleep, but tossed upon my cool couch of palm leaves, unable and unwilling to banish the bright vision of a new, and happy home, for the brave men and fair women of my native land, where we may, without fanatical interference, bring up our sons to emulate the virtues of the wise and good; and our daughters, as the "polished corners of the temple." Just as the glorious sun of the morning had tipped with gold the rich crowns of the "everlasting hills," that surround the valley of Brook Cornelia, we took up our return line of march, and, by taking a more direct route, reached the residence of Sr. Fortes about mid-day. Here we feasted, and rested, until near sun-set, when our canoe was re-loaded, and we began the descent of the Juquiá River.

I returned from this point, and discontinued the explorations, which the generous government of Brazil has afforded me the facilities to prosecute, because I have found a region to which I can, conscientiously, and with enthusiasm advise my countrymen to emigrate.

Nearly four months have elapsed since the foregoing report of my tour in the Province of S. Paulo was written, during which time I have found it necessary to make two voyages from the Capital to our chosen locality, in order to complete, and settle, beyond a peradventure, all the titles to lands, and the boundaries of our community. In short, everything which appertains to the forming of a new settlement. The first of these voyages was without interest, farther than that it served to convince me that a second was unavoidable.

I left Rio de Janeiro on the 11th of May, on this second voyage, on board the fleet little schooner "Third of May," in company with a goodly number of choice companions; among whom, were Mr. Jacob Humbird, of Maryland, Dr. R. M. Davis, of Virginia, and Capt. W. Frank Shippey, of Florida. After a lively sail of three days, we reached Cananeâ, where we were joined by our worthy friend, Major Ernesto D. Street, Inspector-General of the Province of São Paulo. When we reached the region selected for the future homes of our unfortunate Southerners, Mr. Humbird, who is an eminently practical, go-ahead man, was so much pleased, and so well convinced that our labors will result successfully, that he invested largely in the choice fronts on the Ribeira and Juquiá rivers, paying the cash, and giving these sitios into my charge, with instructions to turn them over, at cost, to our people. This I have already done in one instance, in the case of Capt. Shippey, who has gone to work, on a splendid tract of river bottom land, to get ready for his coming relations and friends. After completing all our work on these rivers, passing

Escrituras Publicas, clearing and making the ground for the house your Excellency has ordered to be built, we set out, in company with Inspector-General Street, to explore the region lying between the head-waters of the Juquiá River, and the old town of Sorocaba,—back of the coast range. We found this expedition a rough undertaking, rendered more difficult by four days of incessant rain that pelted us thoroughly, while in the mountains. But we finally got through, making almost the whole journey on foot. After crossing the mountains, I saw specimens of cotton in the field, equal to any I have ever seen in the United States. This is emphatically the cotton-growing region of Brazil, and only needs the appliances of labor and improved culture to make it profitable indeed. Here, also, is an exhaustless supply of mules and horses, where our people can procure their necessary animals, much cheaper than in any part of the United States. I purchased in Sorocaba, two match mules—large and fine, perfectly gentle and tractable—for $35 each, and sent them back for plantation use in the Juquiá valley. I am much gratified that we passed through this region, since it gives us a more practical knowledge of the route for the proposed road, all of which the Inspector-General will doubtless report upon.

From Sorocaba we rode through on horse-back, to the city of São Paulo, in two days—a distance of seventy-two miles. Here we rested one day, took the train for Santos at 6 A. M., and arrived at 11 A. M., just in time to breakfast and go on board the swift steamer S. José, which brought us safely and pleasantly to Rio de Janeiro in about eighteen hours.

And now, Illustrious Sir, that the time nears when I am to return to the land that gave me birth, to superintend the removal of those tried ones to these shores, whose aching hearts crave the repose and security so nobly extended, it seems fitting that I should indicate the course that I propose to pursue. First, then, of all, I do not intend to encourage any one to cast his lot with us, whose moral character, and social status, are not decidedly good. This one rule, closely adhered to, will give us, in all respects, a desirable population. That many of them will be poor, yea, poor in the extreme, is an evil for which we, of the South, are not responsible. In fact, if wordly goods, just now, were made the standard of excellence in the devastated districts of the United States, the poorest would be the best, since, in most instances, men retained their property by sacrificing that which was of far greater value. And further, if my life is spared, to return to this land of my adoption, I shall deem it my duty to warn our people that they may avoid alike those alien croakers, who hang with the tenacity of real parasites, to the vitals of Brazil, whence they draw the means of self-aggrandizement, at the same time they endeavor, parasite-like, by false representations, to smother the young giant that gives them life; and those, who approach under the guise of friendship, professing deepest interest and warmest affection, placing the velvet paw so gently on, that it is not felt, until all of a sudden, it hardens into the stony clutch of the remorseless Shylock. If those of my countrymen, who look to this Empire as their home, immediately, or *in futuro*, do not escape the bewildering fogs and disheartening quicksands, into which these aliens to the commonwealth of Brazil, would lead them on the one hand, and the cunningly arranged traps on the other, baited with "what money they need for the present," it shall be no fault of mine.

With profound sentiments of esteem,

I am, Sir, your obedient Servant,

BALLARD S. DUNN.

CHAPTER XI.

OFFICIAL REPORT OF MESSRS. M'MULLAN AND BOWEN, OF TEXAS, TO THE MINISTER OF AGRICULTURE.

RIO DE JANEIRO, *May* 24, 1866.

To his Excellency the Minister of Agriculture:

EXMO. SR.: The undersigned, after returning their warmest thanks for the many favors received at the hands of your Excellency, and for the facilities afforded them in search of homes for themselves and friends, beg leave to present the following report on the result of their observations, after an experience of five months' almost continual travel in this magnificent and peculiarly favored Empire.

On 9th of January, under arrangements made by order of your Excellency, we went on board the Dom Affonso, accompanied by several other American friends, and all bound for Cananeâ in the Province of São Paulo.

On the morning of the 10th our vessel put to

sea, and on the 13th, at 4 P. M., we dropped anchor in the fine harbor of the ancient village of Cananeâ, having touched at the accustomed points of Ubatuba, São Sebastião, and Santos; the latter of which has a spacious harbor, well situated in a military point of view, and enjoying peculiar advantages commercially.

Santos is destined to be one of the finest cities of the Empire, being the port of an extensive fertile region, soon to be populated by an industrious, intelligent agricultural people, from the Southern States of North America.

Cananeâ is on an island, and near the lower entrance of the Mar Pequeno, a sort of inland sea nearly fifty miles in length, and varying from one and a half to three miles in width, and with sufficient depth for vessels drawing fifteen feet of water.

Cananeâ (or the land of Canaan) is one of the oldest settlements in the Empire; and although quite small at present, it is destined to grow into a place of some importance, enjoying, as it does, an excellent harbor, and with a fertile region in its rear to build it up. Here we met the Inspector-General, Major Street, who very promptly made the necessary arrangements for our penetrating the interior, appointing Mr. Louis Donker Van der Hoff, a very

7*

competent gentleman, at the suggestion of our friend Capt. Buhlaw, to accompany us in our explorations. Among the acquaintances made at Cananeâ were the Delegado and Vigario, both of whom offered us every civility, and seemed anxious that we should establish ourselves in their midst.

After spending several days at this place, on the evening of the 18th we set out on foot for the port, a distance of some three miles, two of which are by land, through a low, generally wet, and very sandy soil, covered with a stunted growth of trees which have barely been able to raise their heads above the thick jungle which mats the earth beneath them. Crossing the interior arm of the Mar Pequeno, about one mile in width, and with a depth sufficient to admit large vessels, we found ourselves at the Port (of the Colony of Cananeâ).

Here we obtained horses, which we mounted, and were soon off in the direction of the colony, over a road which, with very little labor, could be made transitable for all kinds of wagons.

For the first four miles the country very much resembled that traversed in reaching the Port; but, on arriving at the Itapetanga, the whole face and character of the country are changed to a rich mulatto, sticky soil, and a fine, thrifty growth of timber.

The Itapetanga is a beautiful, clear, bold-running creek, flowing over a bed of sand and gravel, and meandering through a fertile valley of four or five hundred yards in width, bounded on either side by lofty hills almost deserving the name of mountains, and covered with an abundance of fine large timber, suitable either for building purposes or furniture. This stream flows into the interior arm of the Mar Pequeno a short distance below the Port (before mentioned), and is navigable for canoes several leagues.

Following up the valley some two and a half miles, we reached the comfortable dwelling of Mr. Van der Hoff, where we stopped for the night. Mr. Van der Hoff is a Dutchman, and lives on the good old "milk and butter" style, *his* being the *only* place in Brazil where we found those excellent (not to say luxurious) articles of food, notwithstanding the peculiar adaptation of the country for them in plenty and to spare at all seasons.

The 19th, being rainy, we spent at Van der Hoff's, feasting on pine-apples, examining the young coffee-trees, which, at two and a half years, were bending under their load of berries, and six or seven kinds of potatoes, one of which has a heavy top not unlike a thrifty collard, and equally as palatable.

On the morning of the 20th we set out early for

the colony, where we arrived in time for breakfast—the Director (Mr. Smith) extending to us a hearty welcome, and offering us the hospitalities of his bountiful board.

The colony is located on the head-waters of the Itapetanga and Pindavina, in a healthy though rather broken country.

From Mr. Smith's house to the Port (before mentioned) it is about twelve miles.

After breakfast we pushed on through the colony, crossing the dividing ridge (before suggested), taking down the Pindavina in the direction of Sr. Francisco Xavier's, the Director himself, our friend Major Totten, and Captain Hanson accompanying us. The Pindavina is a small creek emptying into the Garahú near Xavier's. This gentleman gave us a kind reception, offering us the civilities of his house, which we were thankful to accept after a rather hard trip over a desperate road, and through a rough, hilly country, having made some dozen miles since leaving the house of Director Smith.

On the following morning, accompanied by Sr. Xavier, we took canoe and hastened up the Garahú to the falls, a distance of four miles by water. Major Totten, who is a professional mechanic, seeing the advantages which this place offered for a saw-mill, at once secured it, and within a very short time from this date will (with his associate, Capt. Hanson,) be floating large quantities of excellent lumber down this beautiful stream to the Jacupiranga, and down the latter to the great Ribeira (in all about twenty-five miles by water), whence it will be taken to Iguape (the sea-port).

On the 22d we descended (Major Totten concluding to accompany us) to the newly begun village of Botujurú, a run of twelve miles below Xavier. This place is on the Jacupiranga, six miles below the mouth of the Garahú; and when the country becomes settled, and the commerce will justify it, will be about the head of steamboat navigation on this stream—subsequent investigations developing that, with very little labor, the Jacupiranga may be made navigable thus far for small steamers for at least half the year.

The site of Botujurú is well selected, in the midst of a fertile region, and commands a fine view of the surrounding country.

Leaving this place, we ascended the Jacupiranga, a good canoe run of two days, reaching the great falls. Here, as on the Garahú, is an excellent seat for any amount of machinery, and with plenty of good timber; but, as the valleys are small and the hills high and rugged, we deemed it unsuitable for a large settlement of Americans. So we resolved to retrace our steps, taking a short run up the Bananal (a small confluent of the Jaçupiranga) in the descent, and again reached Botujurú, having been absent four or five days.

The lands in this region are of excellent quality, resembling somewhat the Red River lands of Texas and Louisiana, of the United States, and well situated up to the falls; but the margins of the rivers are all private property.

Before leaving this place, we took a short run up the Canho, a large creek which empties into the Jacupiranga a few hundred yards below the village; but finding the country rough and broken, we resolved to return and shift the base of our explorations to Xiririca on the Ribeira.

Descending the Jacupiranga to the mouth of the Turvo, some seven miles, we ascended the latter a distance of perhaps twelve miles by water, whence we prepared to cross the country on horseback. The Turvo is a small, swift-running creek, winding through a rich and beautiful valley of a quarter of a mile in width, and bounded by ranges of hills often low and undulating. We were much pleased with the valley of the Turvo, but found it all owned and occupied.

We now had a long ride of sixteen miles over

one of the roughest countries we had yet seen, and along a dim trailway, often barely perceivable for the first eight miles; and over this part of the road in particular our party presented quite a novel appearance. Imagine a party of six (including a couple of camaradas to carry baggage) with only two horses in the crowd, and these without bridle or saddle—our blankets answering for the latter, while thongs of bark, tied to the under jaw of the animals, made substitutes for the former.

We afterwards procured two other animals with Brazilian saddles, when we got on quite well, and, after a fatiguing journey, reached the lovely and inviting village of Xiririca, one day and a half after leaving Botujurú.

Here we received a hearty welcome by the Sr. Bernardo José Cabral, who kindly tendered us the hospitalities of his house, and made us feel at home at Xiririca. During the next day we were visited by the principal inhabitants of the place, who offered us every attention that a warm-hearted people could, and expressed a desire that we should find in their *muncipio* a suitable location for ourselves and our friends.

Leaving Xiririca with letters from the Delegado and Sub-delegado, we proceeded up the Ribeira, a distance of some twenty miles, to the mouth of the

Batatal; and ascending this large, rapid-running creek ten or twelve miles, we arrived at the house of Sr. Franco, to whom we bore letters. Here we met with the usual kind reception; and as this was the head of canoe navigation (on account of the falls), this gentleman made arrangements for our pursuing our journey still farther into the interior; so we set out up the Batatal in a good horse-path, clomb a considerable mountain, on the very top of which a very large rosewood tree was pointed out to us, as also a quinine tree, from which latter we pulled a portion of bark, descending into one of the most romantic valleys we had ever seen, in the midst of which dwells with peace and plenty Sr. Franco, son of the old gentleman whose house we had left an hour before.

This valley contains about one hundred and sixty acres of superior land, surrounded on all sides by steep mountains from 1,500 to 2,000 feet high; and the same Batatal skirts the base of the mountains on one side, barely finding an entrance into and out of this romantic place. Here Telemachus might have found an abode suited to his fastidiousness, and desired to wander no more.

At an early hour on the following morning, we set out over the mountains in the direction of the Ariado, a tributary of the Batatal, our clever host accompanying us as guide. This was the roughest work we had yet encountered; for a tall mountain, 2,000 feet high, loomed up before us, standing at an angle of 45°; and our only way of crossing it was to cut our way as we went. After a hard struggle we reached the summit, where we were amazed to find ourselves on an elevated plane, large enough for a considerable farm, and literally matted with large tall cane. One would sooner have imagined himself in the midst of a swamp in the United States than on the top of a tall mountain in Brazil. But this we found to be one of the peculiarities of the country—on the tops of the highest mountains is found the largest cane, while in the valleys it is rarely seen. On the top of this mountain, too, we crossed a large, rippling branch, which finds its way off into the Ariado below, into the valley of which we soon descended.

We found three or four families on the Ariado, and were told that one or two of these were squatters. Following up the margin of the stream some two miles, we reached the house of the Sr. Antonio de Prado. This gentleman and his brother are the outside settlers in this direction. Here we got dinner; and as our friend had just killed a fine yearling buck, we fared sumptuously. He told us this excellent game is abundant in these woods, and he kills them whenever he wishes.

The valley of the Ariado is about five miles long, and from five hundred to seven hundred yards in width, and, like the valleys on most of the small streams, is bounded by tall mountains near the top of one of which our host pointed out a tremendous ledge of rocks, which, he said, were lime—the first of the kind we had yet seen in Brazil, the principal being granite, which seems to form the base of all the mountains in the Empire.

Two miles beyond where we were, the waters turn to the Prado, a large, shoaly river, which empties into the Ribeira a short distance above Iporanga, this place being about twenty miles above the mouth of the Batatal. The situation of the country is such, however, that, the waters of the Batatal and Prado, both coming out of the same side of the same tall mountain, there is no perceivable elevation between, and the valley of the Ariado unites with the valley lands of the waters of the Prado. So, within less than three miles from where we were, we were told by all that there was one of the most magnificent of valleys, which, according to estimates made of distance, must contain twenty-five thousand acres of excellent level land, through the midst of which flow many small streams.

We regretted not penetrating the heart of this magnificent region; but, being worn out with fatigue, being a little unwell, there being no road, and desirous of finding a place a little nearer navigation, we slowly retraced our steps; and when the sun was low in the west we were again at home with our friend on the Batatal, where we had left our canoe the day before.

We were informed that there is plenty of marble (red, blue, and white) on the Batatal and Prado, and that specimens, which had been sent to Rio to be examined, were pronounced No. 1; and certain it is that the lead-mines of Iporanga (all in the same section of country) are among the richest and best in the world.

The valley of the Batatal is small; but from what we saw of the interior, and from information collected from reliable sources, from the superior quality of the land, from the amount and quality of the timber, the fine water-power for machinery, the mineral wealth, the salubrity of the climate—this must become one of the most attractive portions of the Empire; and as the Ribeira is navigable for steamboats to the mouth of the Batatal, there will probably be no portion of this section farther than forty miles from navigation.

The road which the Government is now building from Iporanga to Cananeâ will greatly facilitate the settlement of this very desirable country by industrious, intelligent agriculturists.

Descending the Batatal, we dropped down the Ribeira to one of the farms of the Srs. Guimarães, and with this gentleman ascended the Rio Taquary (a northern tributary of the Ribeira) a distance of more than twenty miles, to the great falls.

The valleys of this stream, like those of the Batatal, are narrow up to the falls; but above these we were told that the mountains recede from the river, leaving an extensive valley region of superior country. These falls are the best for machinery that we have seen in the Empire, and the river affords sufficient water to float a steamboat, were it not for the rapids. Major Totten, who still accompanies us, seeing the value of this place, has taken steps to secure it. His lumber may be floated on flats to the Ribeira, thence to the sea-port, a distance of about one hundred and thirty miles by water. Here there are thousands of superior timber, and the largest cane we have yet seen in our travels in this country, it being quite common to see the reed reaching the enormous height of eighty or ninety feet, with a diameter of four or even five inches.

This cane likes to run up the bodies of the trees for support, where it may be seen reaching out beyond the tallest of them fifteen or twenty feet.

We are satisfied we saw cane on the Taquary

one hundred feet high, with branches (of the same cane) fifty feet long and two inches in diameter, and this, in its turn, would have other branches more than fifteen feet long. In places this tall reed grows so thick that it was impossible to get through it without cutting our road. Our friend Guimarães took great pains to give us all the information in his power, and treated us with true Brazilian hospitality. He is quite a genius, has a considerable amount of machinery, and, under favorable circumstances, would have made a first-class machinist.

Leaving the Taquary, we returned to Xiririca, March 9th, after an absence of six or seven days. We regret having lost the name of our young friend who accompanied us on this week's tour, for he was very attentive, and of great service to us. Before leaving Xiririca, there is a circumstance associated with this name that we deem worthy of mention. On our way up, the Sr. Guerra, this gentleman's wife, and a couple of daughters about grown, met us in the parlor, and soon engaged in conversation with us, asking us many questions about the manners and customs of our native country, and expressing a desire to have some American neighbors. We spent a pleasant evening, and, had it not been for the difference in language, might easily have imagined ourselves in an American family. In the morning, at breakfast, we all ate together at the same table. We mention this circumstance because it was the *first* time we had the pleasure of conversing with the Brazilian ladies.

After taking some refreshments here (at Xiririca), we dropped down to the large fazenda of Sr. Miguel Antonio Jorge, about ten miles. This gentleman met us and told us to make ourselves at home. Miguel Jorge is the largest planter of the Ribeira, owning large quantities of slaves, and probably several hundred thousand acres of land. He has a spacious dwelling, an iron sugar-mill, a saw-mill, grist-mill, distillery, &c., &c.; and is quite fixed, after the Brazilian style. His articles of exportation are rice, and aguardente made from the cane.

Here we saw the first apple-tree, which was loaded with fruit, and we took the liberty to try it, finding it very good, and being satisfied that apples may be raised in this part of the country. We also saw here the cinnamon-tree, of which we took a small twig or two, to exhibit in the United States.

We forgot to mention that at Xiririca we saw the first regular peach-orchard. The trees all looked well; but as it was not "peach-time," we had no opportunity of testing the fruit. It is not uncommon to see one or two of these trees at a place.

On the 10th we rested, Mr. Van der Hoff being a little unwell; and on the 11th, with a letter from our host to Sr. Manoel Alves, at the mouth of the Juquiá, we again began the descent of the Ribeira, with the intention of exploring the Juquiá and its waters. Reaching this place, however, and not finding Sr. Alves at home, and after a delay of nearly a day, we concluded to push on to Iguape, undetermined in our minds where we should next go.

On arriving at this place, we met the Rev. Ballard S. Dunn and Mr. Rousel, the former of whom had already selected lands on the Juquiá; and, from the glowing description which he gave of the country, we resolved to visit it, he kindly volunteering to accompany us.

Here Major Totten left us for Cananeâ, it being mutually agreed upon among us. This is why his name does not appear at the bottom of this paper.

At Iguape we received the usual kind treatment. This is a good large town at the upper end of the Mar Pequeno, and is connected with the Ribeira by a large canal about one mile and three quarters long.

As before mentioned, the Mar Pequeno has

sufficient depth to admit large vessels; but we were informed that the canal from the Ribeira is greatly injuring the channel about the city—a matter worthy of close and serious investigation, after which it may be better to close the entrance next the Mar Pequeno.

The Barra de Coparra, the northern entrance of the Mar Pequeno, is only a short distance above the city; but the bar is said to be constantly changing. Consequently large vessels seek the lower entrance, at Cananeâ, and come up the bay to Iguape. Further investigations, however, may prove that steamers drawing eight or nine feet may always reach Iguape by the northern entrance.

We spent two or three days in the city, during which we have made several valuable acquaintances; and on the morning of the 19th, at an early hour, were off up the Ribeira. Having some business at Botujurú, we took up the Jacupiranga, availing ourselves of the occasion to test the navigability of this stream, our opinion of which we have already given. By water, Botujurú is about forty miles from the mouth of the Jacupiranga.

At Botujurú Mr. Van der Hoff received orders to withdraw from us, having accompanied us for two months. We take pleasure in expressing our satisfaction with the manner in which he fulfilled his mission, and avail ourselves of the present opportunity to return him our sincere thanks.

The lands on the lower Jacupiranga are of fine quality, but perhaps better adapted to the raising of sugar-cane and rice than cotton; but corn does remarkably well on these lands.

Descending to the Ribeira, and ascending this to Ponta Grossa, the lower seat of our friend Miguel Jorge, we again met Rev. Mr. Dunn and Mr. Rousel, and together set out up the Ribeira for the Juquiá.

The latter we found to be a large, deep, bold-running river, and navigable for large steamers, without any obstruction, to the mouth of the São Lourenço, a distance of fifty miles by water. Above this place, by taking out two or three large trees, which might obstruct the channel, the same boat could ascend thirty miles farther; where, on account of the numerous falls, navigation must cease.

At its mouth the Juquiá is about one hundred and fifty yards wide, and gradually narrows down to about fifty or seventy at the head of navigation. The S. Lourenço, the largest tributary of the Juquiá, is also a good large stream; and, as on the upper Juquiá, by removing two or three obstructions, can be made navigable for medium-sized steamers a distance of thirty-five miles, to the mouth of the Itariri.

On the Upper Juquiá and São Lourenço, we found a country that did our hearts good, and made us feel that we had at last found the place we had been looking for so long. There, in this delightful region, we determined to locate, and immediately set about negotiating for a front or two, to insure access from the Government lands in the rear of the river.

This we thought we had done (verbally); but finding so much indefiniteness with regard to lines and titles, we resolved to return to the Capital, and ask your Excellency that a competent person might be appointed, on the part of the Government, to adjust these matters. We were not suspicious of any *intentional* fraud on the part of the people, but were only desirous of seeing our way clear, and of guarding against future contingencies. We greatly feared that our Brazilian friends, seeing the caution with which we proceeded, would misinterpret our motives, and think us "over cautious."

Your Excellency, seeing the consistency of our request, and the importance of the first Americans in the country establishing themselves on a firm and secure basis, was kind enough to grant all we asked.

While on the Juquiá this time, we concluded to make a more thorough examination of the Government lands included in the survey which we had selected, the provisional title to which, by order of your Excellency, we have already received from the Inspector-General.

Proceeding up the São Lourenço half a day's run, to the beautiful site of Sr. Joaquim Pedroso, we stopped for the night; and on the following morning, this gentleman kindly accompanying us, ascended a very short distance, where we took up the Biguá, a distance of some eight miles by water, to the outside settlement. Here we left our canoe and set out up the valley to the "terras devolutas" (Government lands), which we soon reached, and to our great satisfaction found them of very superior quality, well situated, and above all overflow. Here we found lands sufficient for twenty families, and lands that we can recommend to our friends. The Biguá is a beautiful creek flowing over a bed of clean, white sand, with a delightful valley spreading out on each side a distance of from three hundred yards to more than a mile, and this skirted by high hills covered with fine, large timber. The Biguá has two tributaries, both of them with valleys such as we have described.

On the Biguá is nearly the only place where we have seen large cane growing in the valleys; but here it abounds.

After a long, hard walk, we returned to our canoe and stopped for the night.

Early on the following morning we began the descent, and at 10 o'clock were again in the house of our hospitable friend, who had accompanied us in our excursion.

After taking some refreshment, we again began the ascent of the São Lourenço, passing some fine coffee fazendas on the river; and early in the evening were snugly resting under the friendly roof of Sr. Capt. Lui Leite. This gentleman, being well acquainted with the country above, volunteered to accompany us; and on the morning of the 30th of April we were off up the river again.

A pull of two hours carried us to the mouth of the Itariri, the head of steamboat navigation on the Rio São Lourenço. Ascending this large tributary after a hard pull, we stopped on the bank for the night with a clever gentleman; and on the morrow, the 1st of May, we continued our journey, passing the mouth of the Rio de Peixe (Fish river), the numerous falls on the Itariri, and reaching about midday the mouth of the Rio do Azeite (Oil river).

The last is a large, rocky, shoaly creek, and decidedly the clearest, most transparent, and purest water we have ever seen in any country. As small a thing as a pin is as clearly perceivable at a depth of ten feet as though it were on the surface.

We have found Brazil remarkable for good water; but in this particular the Azeite enjoys pre-eminence. We ascended this stream a mile and a half, took up the margin of a small confluent (on foot), and were soon on the Government lands once more.

Here, as on the Azeite and its tributaries, we found a place peculiarly suited to our taste; an extensive level plane of from four to ten miles in width, and twelve or fifteen in length, covered with large, straight timber, and a hundred rivulets dancing over their beds of yellow gold-like sand.

This modern Eden is bounded on the south by lofty mountains, from which it receives its ever-bountiful supply of pure, crystal water; on the north, by the mountains of the Guranhanha. On the west, it unites with the large valley of the Peixe, Government lands also.

When the trifling obstructions before mentioned shall have been removed from the S. Lourenço, the heart of this lovely region will be about twelve miles from steamboat navigation. These lands, we think, will be easier to clear than any others we have seen in the country, being of a loose, yellow loam, and with plenty of sand to make them pleasant to cultivate.

Immediately on the rivers Juquiá and Ribeira, the lands often overflow, and occasionally have some wet lands back; but here we have none of these things to contend against, the lands being dry and always above overflow.

This, the 1st of May, was the happiest day we had spent in the Empire; we felt that our hopes were realized, that the great Giver of all good had blessed our honest endeavors to find and secure homes for a brave but unfortunate people.

Here the homeless may find a home, and the outcast a "resting-place, with none to molest or make him afraid." Here are lands equal to any in the world and within three or four days' run from the great Capital of the nation, a climate unsurpassed, neither hot nor cold, and where frost is never known, water as cold as the mountain spring, and so equally distributed as to allow almost every man to run his plantation machinery by it.

Here almost everything grows, and grows well, too, that is calculated to minister to the health and comfort, not to say luxury, of man. Among these we might enumerate corn, sugar-cane, beans, peas, potatoes, coffee, tea, pepper, ginger, peaches, oranges, lemons, limes, bananas, plantains, figs, pine apples, grapes, guyavas, arasas, and many other things.

Apples, wheat, and cotton, have not been tried on any considerable scale; but we have talked with a man that planted a small portion of the second article, and he said it matured well.

We have seen some fine specimens of cotton grown on the Ribeira, and in other sections of this part of the country; but some American farmers are fearful that there is too much rain for it to open well. But this is a matter soon to be tested by ourselves and others. Certain it is, that the stock is thrifty, and the bolls the largest we have ever seen.

On the day following, 2d May, we returned with our generous host to his house; and the next morning were off down the river to our new home on the Juquiá; whence, after a few days, we descended to Iguape again, having spent nearly five months in exploring one of the richest regions of earth.

Before leaving the Ribeira, we must say something of this great body of water. This is a large, deep river, from two hundred to five hundred yards in width, and drains an extensive, fertile country. Its general direction is a fraction north of east, and empties into the sea about twenty miles above Iguape. It has a bad mouth, on account of the tremendous breakers, there being no bay for protection; but barks are passing in and out every week. Large steamers can ascend to Xiririca, and by removing a few rocks which might obstruct the channel, can reach the mouth of the Batatal, about one hundred and fifty miles from Iguape. Above this there is plenty of water, but the numerous shoals will probably forever impede navigation. The lower Ribeira lands are not suitable for persons of small capital; but for wealthy planters who wish to engage in the sugar business, we know of no other place in the world that would suit them better. The Upper Ribeira is truly a desirable country.

The banks of all these streams are covered with capim (the noblest of the grasses), a kind of soft cane (resembling sugar-cane somewhat), and large quantities of the castor bean (palma christi).

We saw but few plants or woods like those in the United States; and those which have the same name differ very much in appearance; as, for instance, the cedar of Brazil is a large, smooth, straight-bodied tree, often much more than one hundred feet high, and the leaves very much resembling in appearance those of the walnut; while, in the United States this tree has a scrubby appearance, and is generally very knotty. The

Brazilian cedar is a much more firm, solid wood, and admits of fine polish.

The birds, too, of this country, differ very much from those of North America; being generally more beautiful, and often decorated by a rich plumage of variegated hues. We often saw the splendid toucano, one of the most beautiful of birds; and were rarely out of hearing of the grating noise of the paroquits. On the Upper Juquiá, we saw droves of parrots; and all the mountains are said to abound with monkeys. The anta (often weighing seven or eight hundred pounds) and the Capivari (a kind of river hog) are found on the rivers and low lands in great abundance, and deer are numerous.

The large grazing ant, which often makes such ravages on the plants and fruits in some of the northern provinces, is hardly to be seen anywhere we have been.

Mosquitoes trouble the people in the woods and on the low lands, and *bixo* (a sort of screw-worm) trouble cattle; but clear off the timber and both disappear.

There is probably no other country in the world where domestic fowls do so well as in Brazil; and where perpetual spring reigns, stock of all kinds can do well. Droughts, which often visit the western portion of the United States, are unknown here to the oldest inhabitants.

A kind of rice-bird was pointed out to us which sometimes has been known to trouble this grain; but this is only a rare occurrence; and all in all, we believe Brazil has fewer annoyances (except bad roads) than any other country in the world.

In fact, there is not another nation under heaven which contains so many of the elements of greatness *within itself* as Brazil. In point of climate, soil, good water, navigable rivers, water-powers, *we stand without a parallel.* We have gold, silver, iron, platina, lead, copper, coal, granite, marble; and, in fact, *everything* that could be desired, except a speedy development of these inexhaustible resources of wealth and power.

We have the best system of government known to man; while it combines all the elements of strength requisite to insure its stability against *every* emergency, it *guarantees* PRACTICAL EQUALITY to ALL its citizens, and administers justice with a firm and willing hand. We have a monarchy (thank God!) in name, and a TRUE *Republic* in practice; and under the wise administration of our good Emperor, our destiny must be onward and upward to a degree of prosperity unknown to other countries.

If the state of agriculture among us at present is backward and antiquated, our people are willing and desirous to improve. They say if the improved mode of culture used by the Americans beats theirs, they too will plow their land, and fell their timber with Collins' axes. "If you prove to us that the valley lands will produce more than the mountain sides, we too will come down and reap the more abundant harvest."

With many prayers for your Excellency's health, and for a long life of future usefulness in your zealous endeavors to promote your country's good, we beg leave to subscribe ourselves,

Your Excellency's obliged, obedient Servants,

Frank M. Mullen,

William Bowen.

CHAPTER XII.

OFFICIAL REPORT OF DR. J. M. F. GASTON, OF SOUTH CAROLINA, TO THE MINISTER OF AGRICULTURE.

In compliance with my wish to examine the lands of the province of São Paulo, the facilities for so doing were furnished under the directions of your Excellency, by the worthy President of the same; and with the kind co-operation and generous assistance of private individuals I have visited a large portion of its territory.

A daily record of observations from the outset to the close of each tour, embracing a period nearly of four months has been accurately kept for the information of those who await my report: and I beg leave respectfully to present for the consideration of your Excellency this statement of the general results of my examination.

For the purposes of description, the following division of land is recognized, viz., Volcanic land

(Terra Rocha), Red land (Terra Vermelha), Dark land (Terra Preta), and light land (Terra Branca). A further distinction of land, results from the predominance of clay (Barro), sand (Arêa), shell (Concha) and decomposed vegetable matter (Vegetable podre) which are combined in various proportions, with other elements in different specimens of soil.

The lands which consist of the dark purple volcanic earth, known as Terra Rocha, are of a homogenous constitution, and extend for a great depth, without perceptible change of the soil. The localities in which this land is found, are more elevated than their surrounding; and are supposed to be the result of some convulsion of nature in a former period of the history of the world.

The presence of iron stone (Pedra de Ferro) is observed to a greater or less extent, in almost every specimen of this land; and when it does not prevail to an extent to hinder cultivation, or prevent the proper growth of plants, it is regarded as a favorable indication.

This particular variety of land, has attracted my attention, especially, as there is no soil in the United States corresponding to it, or having any of its characteristics. It is a distinct well-defined formation, and yet among those familiar with its properties several grades are recognized in regard to productiveness.

The red land (Terra Vermelha) bears a great resemblance in color, under particular circumstances, to that already described, but for the most part does not incline so much to the purple color. In its constitution it is not so loose and loamy as the Terra Rocha; but it assumes more the nature of the red clay lands with which we are familiar in the United States and is remarkably compact and firm.

I have observed a channel for the passage of a rapid little stream of water, through this kind of land and it seemed to make scarcely any impression upon it.

The dark land, (Terra Preta) is found in some places apparently without admixture with vegetable elements, and in such situation has its color from some sulphureous or carbonaceous ingredient of the soil, which may or may not disappear under the process of washing according to the particular combination into which it enters.

The greater part however of the dark land that is valuable for agricultural purposes is composed principally of decayed vegetable mould or compost resulting from the gradual decomposition of deposits from the trees, herbs, etc., which have grown upon the land. This becomes incorporated with other elements and constitutes a soil of great productiveness for a few years, but to be permanently useful it must rest upon a basis of other articles, that will continue to impart vitality when the strength of the vegetable matter declines. Such a foundation is afforded by some specimens of clay (Barro) which prevents the percolation of the extract, favored by the frequent passage of water through this surface formation and preserves the land in a serviceable condition for a series of years.

That form of land, known as Terra Branca is of a light aspect from the large proportion of white sand which is intermixed with the soil, and is usually little else than sand mingled with a greater or less amount of vegetable matter. When the white element predominates, it becomes to that extent sterile, and it may always be taken for granted, that it is little suited for agricultural purposes when the sand is found to continue for any considerable depth below the surface. A small proportion of sand is useful in the composition of a soil for the purpose of promoting the agglutination of the more adhesive particles of earthy substances. But the limit of utility for sand is confined to this object as it cannot by any possibility promote within itself the growth of any vegetation.

In some instances the presence of decomposed

Shell imparts an aspect to lands somewhat similar to that of sand, but upon particular examination it will be found to have proportions of a very different nature. When shell is found united with a proper portion of clay (barro) and sand a combination results that is very favorable to the growth of some plants, and an artificial soil may be thus produced which becomes very useful. The marl of fossil remains should not remain unprofitable.

These elements of the soil, combined in different proportions, constitute most of the lands which have been examined; and being now recognized they may be referred to understandingly, in my special descriptions of the several localities of this province.

Preparatory however to entering upon any details I have to remark that the territory is divided into forest land (matta virgem), open plain land (Campo), and secondary forest (capoeira), each of which is diversified by the particular growth and the nature of the soil.

The forest lands are for the most part superior to the open plains, and yet embrace soil of very different aspects and properties. From the rich purple terra rocha, to the poor and sandy terra branca, may be found in different forests of the province. There is a form of forest land found frequently in the midst of campos, that has the most inferior type of soil upon which trees are ever found to grow. Again we sometimes have seen the primeval fruit upon a soil of the richest kind of terra rocha with a large body of campo land that would scarcely produce anything, in close proximity to each other. It is a striking peculiarity of this region that soils of the most characteristic difference in their qualities, and with the most dissimilar growths, are found in juxta-position, presenting a correct exemplification of the oasis in the desert.

There is a great variety of trees found in the different forests, and yet I have not encountered a single specimen of the native trees of the United States growing spontaneously in the woods of this province. On the other hand I have been pleased to find many of the fruit trees here that I have been familiar with before, and some of them apparently growing vigorously, yet not affording fruit in every instance of equal size and flavor with those of the United States. In this category stands the apple, the peach and the quince, while figs and grapes seem to flourish here quite as well as any I have seen elsewhere. In the midst of native wilds of the forest, in many portions of the province, are found trees bearing the most delicious fruits and among them the most prized is the sweet Jaboticaba.

The open plain (Campo) land has usually a

surface that approaches a level, or is slightly undulating, and without trees of any magnitude.

Some portions of the campos have a stinted and scattered growth of scrubby looking trees, while in others a growth of shrubby, and dwarf fruit trees is observed to occupy the ground; but by far the largest extent of this kind of territory is found with a growth of more or less grass upon it. There is quite a diversity in the different grasses produced by various specimens of campos, some being well suited to the use of animals, while others are not eaten or tend very little to promote nutrition.

The fruit trees found in the campo are for the most part diminutive types of larger trees which are found in lands of different quality. The fruits are generally very palatable, and I was specially pleased with the Cajú, which is of a slightly acid taste, affording a very agreeable refreshing drink, when used as lemonade with a little sugar and water.

In addition to these fruits there are numerous medicinal plants in the campos, belonging to the standard Materia Medica, while others are adapted especially to the disorders of the country, or to the relief of bites by venomous reptiles. Where the fruits and medicinal plants are found, the ground is occupied by them to the exclusion of most other things. On the other hand, when the grass prevails, very little else is found upon the surface, even in patches where it failed to grow.

This peculiar adaption of certain portions of the ground to the growth of particular natural products must strike all with surprise who are not familiar with this country: and we are at a loss to explain the condition of these dwarf trees in a soil that grows other trees, when planted, of much larger size.

In different localities I have seen growing upon the campo soil, with fine proportions, the Figueira Grande, the Pina and Ximbo. Were there no trees of any kind upon these campos, it might be inferred that no seed had been deposited in the soil, but finding these trees of dwarf proportions, presents a very peculiar and interesting problem.

It is true that the soil is usually of the poorest order, when this is observed, and it may be that the planting of other trees in this identical soil, would not secure any more favorable result.

CULTIVATION OF THE SOIL.

The culture of the land in all parts visited is performed with the hoe exclusively, and though improvements of various kinds are observed in the mechanical department, there seems to be very little disposition to resort to the plow as a more thorough and efficient process of cultivation.

Though a good yield is secured without it we may calculate that it would be increased at least one half more by the proper use of this important implement of the planter in the United States. Throughout this wealthy province I saw but three persons who used the plow at all and it was limited in their cases to a very narrow sphere, being employed simply to prepare the ground for planting and not used subsequently for the treatment of the growing plant. Could anything I may say induce the adoption of plow-culture for the cotton that is now engaging so much of the attention of planters in this Province, it would serve to enhance greatly the value of this crop, and at the same time lessen the actual amount of labor by those working the lands.

Where the ground is laid out in right lines by the plow, preparatory to planting, it simplifies very much the labor of planting, and the ground being deeply and thoroughly loosened up, gives the young plant a better prospect for taking root in the earth.

I observe but few persons who realize the importance of stirring the soil as a means of promoting the growth of what may be planted, and in most instances cotton and corn are allowed to grow in such close juxta-position as materially to interfere with the supply of nutriment from the soil, and the action of the atmosphere as an invigorating agent.

The cotton plant especially requires a free circulation of air, and the full operation of the same upon every part; and when crowded with three or four stalks in one place, this influence cannot be received. It is not an uncommon thing to see six stalks of corn growing in one spot, which run up tall and slim, without that stamina which is requisite to produce the largest and best ears of corn. Two stalks in a hill at the same distance may occasionally be seen, and the improvement in the result is so evident that I am surprised this mode of culture should be continued by intelligent planters of this country.

GAME.

As to the amount of game and wild animals in the different parts of the province, I have been pleased to learn that the deer, which is the most desirable, is the most abundant, and though the yelp of the dogs has been frequently heard in chase of this animal, if I am to judge by my having seen none upon the tables of the fazendas, I must infer that they are very seldom caught.

The small forest hog is another excellent species of game that is found in abundance; and having been more fortunate in regard to it, I can testify that the flesh is sweet and delicate, being superior and quite different from the domestic hog. I have also eaten the flesh of the Paca, which is considered among the best of the denizens of the forest, yet it was not so palatable to my taste as that spoken of in the previous paragraph.

Among the things eaten here is a large lizard that corresponds in appearance and proportions to a young alligator, being frequently two and a half feet long. I have seen the flesh dressed, and it presented a very nice aspect, yet the associations in my mind with the class of reptiles, render this animal by no means desirable as a part of my bill of fare. It is said to be a foe to the Cobra, which is known to be the most venomous of reptiles, and in their conflicts the lizard is always the victor, killing its antagonist very promptly. These large lizards are very numerous in all parts of the province, and this perhaps explains the comparative scarcity of the cobra, of which but two have been seen throughout my tours. These were both large, and resembled very much the rattlesnake which is very common in the United States, and equally venomous as the cobra. I encountered these venomous serpents in crossing the Serra Paranapiaca, and my Camarada succeeded in killing both. It was a region suited to all that is disagreeable, as mortal man never perhaps travelled, with greater inconveniences and hazards of life and limb, than I brooked in my desperate resolve to cross this almost impassable Serra.

The Tapir is another fine species of game found here, and being of the proportions of an ox, it affords quite a feast when one is captured in the chase.

In the dense unpopulated parts they are still said to be very abundant, and it is considered one of the most exciting exercises of the sportsman to get a pack of dogs after this animal.

Tigers are said to be frequent in most of the woods, and I saw several skins, but they are for the most part small, and not prone to do mischief.

Monkeys likewise abound, but are shy and keep concealed.

CONFIGURATION, AND QUALITY OF LANDS.

In considering the qualities and configuration of the lands in this province, they may be appropriately divided into four distinct sections:

First.—The coast lands lying adjacent to Santos, Conceição, Cananeâ, and Iguape.

Second.—The table lands lying adjacent to Campinas, Limeira, Rio Claro, Araraquara, Brotas, Jahú, and Botacutú.

Third.—The mixed lands lying adjacent to São Paulo, Jundiahy, Itú, Porto Felix, Sorocaba, Itapeninga, and Paranapanema.

Fourth.—The river lands lying adjacent to Yporanga and Xiririca, and located upon the Ribeira de Iguape and its tributaries.

Though fully aware that there is not that uniformity of soil or allocation, in any one of these sections, which will render any general description applicable to all the parts, yet there is a conformity to a standard in type of land, that warrants the distinction here made.

There are likewise natural limitations in the structure of the serras, and the arrangement of the water courses, which further favor this grouping of parts together, and at the same time separating them from others more allied to each other.

That portion of territory styled *Coast land* lies between the sea and the crest of a serra, or high range of hills, extending with little interruption from one extremity to the other of region indicated. The soil has two distinct aspects: that of the low, flat and moist land, extending from the edge of the water to the foot of the serra; and the other being an elevated slope constituting the side of the serra looking towards the sea. The former consists, for the most part, of sand with decayed vegetable matter, and in some parts having an admixture of rotten shell or marl. When the vegetable matter predominates, it is of a dark color, and in most parts is well suited to the growth of rice. In such places as the two formation elements are united favorably with the sand, the character of the soil is improved, and the yield increased.

The more elevated slope of the serra has more of the clay basis, and with some sand and vegetable matter, constitutes in parts a soil upon which corn and cotton grow moderately well. When the washings from the hill sides become mixed with the less consistent materials of the flat below, a very decided improvement is observed, and sugar cane finds an appropriate place. A small experiment of bringing down the clay soil of the hill side, and incorporating it with the moist sandy soil of the low land, would satisfy those cultivating these lands of its advantages; and no labor that can be bestowed upon this soil, would be so likely to prove remunerative to the agriculturist.

On the flat marshy land of this section, the mangue-bravo and the mangue-manso grow in great abundance, the bark of the former, and the leaves of the latter, being used extensively for tanning leather. There are trees of various kinds growing upon the slopes of the serra, which are well suited to domestic purposes and yet but little used.

In the *second* section the diversity of soil, and the contrast in the general aspects of the country is particularly striking; the most fertile lands being in close contact with the most sterile; and the most exuberant vegetation, with trees of the greatest magnitude, covering the former; while the latter is very sparsely supplied with a growth of low scrubby trees and coarse grass. The matta virgem lands are chiefly of the variety of terra rocha, and of the very best quality; but there are also found large bodies of terra branca, covered with a growth of large trees, and some of the most useful kinds abound in this section.

In the district of Limeira I was favored with the inspection of 36 different specimens of wood grown there and considered valuable for building or the construction of various articles. Among other valuable trees of this section the Avindiaba is abundant, and is considered the most durable when exposed to the weather, or placed partly in the earth.

In the terra rocha lands the Páo-de-alho and the Figueira-branca are found associated in large number and of huge proportions, and are considered the best indications of fertility of soil.

The campo lands of this section are of two distinct aspects, terra vermelha, and terra branca, the former having a place in the neighborhood of Araraquara, while the latter is found near Rio Claro and Brotas, and is very inferior either for grazing or for cultivation. The red campos produce in many places fine grass, and quite a variety of fruits and medicinal plants, but so far as was observed there has been very little attempted in cultivating these lands.

It is said by almost every planter, that the use of the plow would secure a yield from these red campos but my doubts of their productiveness, without the use of manure, can only be removed by a successful experiment in their cultivation. The indigo grows spontaneously upon this soil, and doubtless its systematic cultivation, and manufacture, would prove very profitable.

In various portions of this section, where the terra rocha prevails, the coffee is grown upon a magnificent scale, and the appliances for treating it have been carried to the greatest perfection. The sugar cane has also received much attention in former years, and extensive establishments for its manufacture into sugar, syrup or rum have been in operation very successfully.

One of the greatest difficulties in the remote part of this section is the transportation of products to a market, and yet with the remarkable fertility of the soil, the population are enjoying a prosperity which is not found elsewhere. For many things a market has been found in neighboring parts of the province; but now that cotton is cultivated it is very important that better means of transportation shall be provided; and it is thought to be entirely practicable to extend the line of railroad towards Araraquara, thus giving that rich country an outlet for its products. The cotton crop of that region is likely to be very important, as a yield of 2,400 pounds to the acre was reported to me from one field, and this far exceeds the best results of cotton growing in the United States. Not only is the soil here well adapted to cotton, but there is a decided advantage in the continuous growth of the plant from year to year, whereas in the United States it is killed annually by the frost and the crop cut short.

The facilities for water are abundant in all parts of this section, and scarcely is a house found without some mechanical operation by the supply of water. Saw mills, and small mills for grinding corn, are very common, while those for cotton are also introduced in some places.

The Monjola is an institution of former days, to which many of the inhabitants still adhere most pertinaciously for the fabrication of farinha and big hominy.

The pleasant associations with this section have been marred by the frequent exhibition of persons laboring under that deformity of the neck known technically as bronchocele (papo), and not only are females of all ages laboring under it, but males in like manner are found with it to a large extent. It seems to be more prevalent with those living near the serras, and is perhaps attributable in some measure to the mode of living, as well as to the drinking of the water from these elevated mineral reservoirs. The extensive prevalence of this affection at the foot of the Alps has been assigned to drinking snow water, but in the serras of Brazil some other agent induces it, and most likely it is from a similar cause in each location, connected with the traces of volcanic minerals in these mountain elevations.

Leprosy is also observed to some extent, and is one of the most offensive diseases of the skin and other tissues. In other respects the health of this section is very good.

In the *third* section of our division of the lands, there is an admixture of campo and matta lands in some parts, inducing a sort of mean strength of soil that falls far short of thé prime quality of land in the former section. In other parts the campos prevail and there are large undulating plains covered with green grass that serves well to support the cattle that are seen grazing upon them. When a portion of woodland is observed in connection with these plains it partakes of the nature of those hillocks and irregular elevations, which characterize the forest lands in other parts of this section. The soil is for the most part of a dark grey aspect, resulting from the admixture of sand with decomposed vegetable matter, and there is underneath this usually a basis of light blueish clay, which assumes nearly an ash color in its union with the superficial soil.

The color of this clay varies considerably in various specimens of this land, but it all has more or less sand incorporated with it, and thus is not very liable to become hard and impervious to the roots of plants. Though the lands of this section are not endowed with the strength or the permanency of those previously described they have proved to be well adapted to the culture of cotton. Many plantations which were regarded as quite unprofitable prior to the introduction of the cotton, are now growing the plant successfully; and I was favored with a visit to a cotton field near Sorocaba, that promises to make a yield little inferior to the finest lands seen elsewhere.

In all parts where the cotton has received a fair trial upon the average lands of this section the result has been favorable; and the regions adjacent to Itú and Porto Feliz are likely to have new life infused into the agriculturists by their success in growing this plant. Even in the remote districts of Itapetininga and Paranapanema, the cotton is attracting attention, and a few persons have already tested the practicability of producing a fair article. It is likely to remunerate well the laborer at present prices, even with the long distance, and the high tariff charged for transportation to Santos. This region of country seems to be more naturally supplied with an outlet by the Ribeira, and the road which has been undertaken to Sete Barras, would afford an important line of communication, yet at present it is considered entirely impracticable even for pack mules.

The water power in this section is brought into requisition at a few places only, and cotton gins were found running by steam at Itú and Sorocaba; while at Itapetininga the most ludicrous display of motive power the world has ever produced, was witnessed in the operation of a treadmill worked by three men, for the ginning cotton.

There is within four miles of Itú an extraordinary combination of facilities for the erection of machinery, afforded by the (Salto) fall of water in the river Tieté; and if an enterprising company would establish a cotton factory at that point, it might receive all the crude material from the river below, as it is navigable in large canoes up to this place. A direct road from this place to the railroad at Jundiahy, or wherever it should be found most practicable, would give at once an outlet to all its fabrics; and the interest of this section materially promoted, while the owners would certainly obtain a good return for the capital invested.

The lands and climate in the vicinity of Itú seem to be well suited to the production of fruits and grapes, and the specimens imported from the United States are yielding very satisfactorily.

The Quarry of slate or flag stone near Itú is a most interesting display of nature's works, and the beautiful pavements of the town show how admirably adapted it is to a more extended usefulness, could any economical means of transportation be devised to convey it to other parts of the country. Such a mass of flag stone convenient to any large city would be a valuable acquisition, whereas now it lies almost useless.

Nothing has been encountered in this section of greater importance than the grand reservoir of Iron ore at Ypanema, which contains 80 per cent. of metal of the best quality that can be found in any country; and though the Government is now once more making an effort to bring their appliances into successful operation, perhaps all will concur in the opinion that a private organization, with a large capital, would be more likely to secure the desired result. If an energetic company were permitted to take the place, with some assistance from the Government, their individual interests would infuse an energy into the enterprise which is not likely to attend any plan adopted by the Government. It is said to be but fifteen leagues to the Juquiá, and that the route may be made practicable for wagons, carts, etc.

The *fourth*, and last division of territory, consisting of the lands lying upon the Ribeira de Iguape and its tributaries, is included between the Serra de Cadeias which bounds the coast lands, and the Serra Paranapiaca, which separates this from the third section. The lands are in many places very irregular, and in some parts almost mountainous, but descending from Yporanga towards Xiririca, the conformation of the surface improves, and in passing across the country towards Cananeâ it even assumes the character of an undulating plain.

The forest lands prevail throughout this entire section, there being no campos found within its limits, and the original growth is found in all parts, excepting near the Ribeira, where the larger tracts of land were formerly planted, but subsequently allowed to lie idle, and have produced a secondary forest. The trees are not generally so large as those observed in the rich terra rocha of the second section, but still there are many of immense proportions, and providing materials for canoes that will carry two thousand pounds of freight to market. The Canella Preta, Araribá, Peroba and Batalha are some of the most useful for canoes.

The soil immediately upon the banks of the Ribeira is a mass of rich loam, formed by the gradual decomposition of earth and vegetable matter, with very little sand. It presents very much the appearance of wet ashes, with a depth usually of five or six feet upon the immediate margin. From the mouth of the Juquiá up to the Juquary, a distance of twenty-five miles, the banks of the Ribeira are high and in many places perpendicular. But in others they have a slight inclination, which is covered with the most luxuriant (capim) grass.

It is very rare that inundations occur in this region, and scarcely ever does the river go beyond the banks above Xiririca. In the lower lands, nearer to Iguape, the water is said to cover large tracts of country when rains cause a great increase in the Ribeira; and the limit of the desirable region for cultivation does not descend much below the mouth of the Paraqueira river, but a short distance below the Jacupiranga, on the south side of the Ribeira.

In passing from the Ribeira to the interior lands, quite a different soil is observed, and with various modifications, as it is elevated or low land.

Upon the hills the surface presents usually a dark aspect, from the admixture of decayed vegetable matter with the other ingredients of the soil, and having in most specimens some sand mingled with it. This is usually from three to four inches thick, and beneath is found a more compact mulatto soil, with the predominating element of clay commingled with the sand. This presents a consistent uniform mass, and is a good basis for the more perishable superstructure of vegetable loam. It is found to support vegetation well, when all the superficial dark soil has been removed, and though the primary yield of the earth is evidently better this evidence of stamina in the dark strata is important for the growth of such articles as send roots deeply in the earth. In the level places near the smaller streams, and in the valleys between the hills, there is more of the vegetable mould in the soil, and the clay basis seems to be more variable in color, being of a light blue aspect in many situations. It does not indicate a soil so permanent, or so fertile, as that of more elevated positions, and yet corn and rice grow well in these situations.

The hills slope gradually down to these level plains, but the line of demarcation in the soil is generally very well defined, manifesting an original difference in the constituent elements of the land.

The territory lying above the town of Xiririca and adjacent to the waters of the Ribeira Jaquary, presents an elevated tract of land varied by hills, plains and valleys, which embodies all the conditions of a desirable location, and is adapted to the growth of all the staples of the country. In connection with other articles the coffee was there seen growing most satisfactorily, and the trees were heavily laden with fruit. The reports of the culture of coffee in this region were not based upon any systematic records, yet they indicated a favorable result of the experiments that have been thus far made, and from my own observation, I am inclined to think that coffee may be successfully cultivated in this region of country near Xiririca.

Corn has long been a staple commodity, and the growing crops present a good appearance. The cotton has been planted by a few persons with good results, and the culture is now being much extended.

The communication with this section is attended with less difficulty than any of the others, and the transportation by canoes to Iguape is much cheaper than it would be by land, and thence products may go either to Santos or Rio de Janeiro with comparatively small outlay for freight.

Independent of the large bodies of public lands in this section, which are available, there are several square leagues of private lands, lying parallel with the Ribeira, at an average distance of one league from it, which may be purchased by emigrants upon reasonable terms, these lands have some portions under cultivation, and a number of houses located upon them, with lines of communication with the river at three points, one about twelve miles below. Upon each of these lines, roads might be constructed that would serve for wagons and carts, and the assistance of the Government in this matter would render these lands desirable for the first settlement of emigrants, as private arrangements can be made satisfactorily for their immediate occupation.

The lands of the Government lying adjacent to these, and between them and Cananeâ, extending towards Paraná, will accommodate an immense population, and if it should meet the views of our people to settle upon these lands, lines of communication through this territory become at once necessary. A good wagon road from Xiririca to the port of the Colony of Cananeâ would perhaps be most in demand at the outset, and this is indicated even in advance of settlement so that the household furniture and farming implements of emigrants locating near this line, may be transported to their destination. There being steam navigation to both of these points, a practicable public road connecting these would enable those who might locate upon either side of it, to communicate with Xiririca, or with the port of Cananeâ, as might be most convenient to them, and will be required primarily for the passage of emigrants and the transportation of their household supplies, as well as the articles necessary for cultivating the ground and treating its products. But secondarily its importance is greatly enhanced by affording an outlet for the various commodities which may be sent to market from this fertile region of country lying between these places. The route indicated is thought by engineers to be very favorable for the location of a good wagon road, and should Your Excellency think proper to authorize it to be made forthwith, it would constitute an important recommendation of this section for the settlement of emigrants from the southern part of the United States of America.

In addition to the advantage of procuring lands at small cost from the Government, the facility of reaching by water communication renders the transportation to and from this section much less expensive, than in situations where it is necessary to use pack mules, and the promptness of communication with other parts is also a matter of much moment in the settlement of a country.

Families may reach either Cananeâ or Xiririca by steamer, taking all their utensils with them, and with roads leading into the interior they may be domesticated in a few days after arrival.

As to the health of all this country, after leaving the coast it is unquestionably good. Those residing low down upon the Ribeira and in the vicinity of Iguape and Cananeâ, are not likely to have good health, but that low land is not included in the territory indicated as appropriate for our people, and it does not in any way affect the salubrity of the more elevated lands. The aspect of the people living even immediately upon the banks of the rivers in the vicinity of Xiririca is healthy and vigorous, and the more rapid flow of the water, with the general configuration of the country, indicates an entire exemption from all miasmatic diseases. The climate in this locality is more genial than a more northern latitude and the elevation of the lands affords entire exemption from that dampness of the atmosphere which is found in low situations. Intermittent fever is unknown in this locality.

None of those swellings of the neck known as papo are found here. And no instance of leprosy has been seen or heard of in this entire section. Whether these affections result from improper diet and poor living, from bad water or from climate, it is certainly preferable for families to locate where they do not exist, and thus have the assurance that the influence which produces them is not in operation.

Good lands, good climate, good means of transportation, and good health, are the inducements for locating in this section of the country, and I doubt whether a more favorable combination can be found elsewhere.

I have the honor to express my obligation to Your Excellency and also to the President of the Province of São Paulo, for the consideration extended to me personally, and for the means afforded for examining this country. My thanks are respectfully returned for the same. I am pleased likewise to acknowledge the receipt of many favors from private persons which have greatly facilitated my object, and for which I feel truly grateful. With sentiments of the greatest respect, I am your obliged and obedient servant,

J. M. F. Gastin.

CHAPTER XIII.

THE LABOR QUESTION.

To Mr. Jacob Humbird, of Maryland, a resident of Brazil, and an active friend of such Southerners, as intend to emigrate to that country, the following sensible article, on the vital subject of labor, was addressed. This gentleman has been for many years, largely, and successfully engaged in railroad building: consequently, he is eminently competent, from long experience, to judge of any system of labor, and of all systems, relatively considered.

I am aware of the fact, that he fully endorses the views expressed in the letter, as printed below.

It is to his brain, and energy, that Brazil is indebted, for the completion of a large portion of that almost impossible enterprise, the Dom Pedro Segunda Railroad. This road is intended to connect Rio de Janeiro, the capital of the Empire, with the rich interior Province of Minas (mines). A large portion, as I said before, and the most difficult of all, has been completed by Mr. Humbird: and the survey, for a much greater extension, is now going forward. B. S. D.

" To Jacob Humbird Esq.

" My Dear Sir: I must, as you well know, hold you entirely responsible for the translation and publication in English of the following letter, which I originally wrote in Portuguese, without the slightest intention of its being read in any other language, and scarcely, indeed, beyond our Province of São Paulo.

" When you lately visited us here, however, you expressed a lively interest in its contents, as having reference to a certain new phase which has developed itself in your own country, and a certain movement which is being made by many of your friends and countrymen with a view to establish for themselves a home in the splendid climate, and on the prolific soil of this Province. Actuated by this feeling, you asked, and afterwards indeed pressed me for a translation of my letter, in order that you might send it for publication to Baltimore, and thus to a certain extent make the public in the Southern States even more acquainted with certain facts probably already known to some of them through those of your countrymen who have been visiting these regions. I felt that I could not refuse you, firstly, because I was anxious to conform with your wishes, so kindly expressed to me, and secondly, because I am very anxious to do everything in my power to make those who are already resolved on emigration somewhere, aware of what a really happy future is abundantly open to them here. I am quite confident that any families coming from the Southern States to Brazil, will be best satisfied by coming to this Province, because it so unquestionably unites fertility with salubrity, and offers an entirely new field for their well-known cultivation of the cotton plant.

"In my short, and (so far as the foreigner is concerned) very imperfect letter, I have sufficiently touched upon this latter subject to excite attention, and it will be observed that what I say is not only derived from actual facts already existing in this Province, but from actual observations made to me by the American planters whom I accompanied. Nor do I shrink from declaring strongly the urgent necessity for roads. I have done this in connection with our own great enterprise, seeking to arouse public opinion and public action on the subject, in a country where all are too apt to lie still and cry aloud to the Government. This absence of good roads, after all, to an enterprising race, such as yours and mine, is but a comparatively small matter to remedy. The great fact for your friends to bear in mind is that they have got the cotton. If the roads were here, and the cotton produce had to be tried and proved, that reverse of the picture would be far more serious; but, in truth, the cotton is here, and we only want the roads. The immigration of any considerable number of your North-American families here would very soon put all this in order, and of one thing towards that end I feel very confident viz.: that any reasonable amount of money would be readily forthcoming in England, to advance railways or tramways throughout the country, were it once well-known that a substantial immigration from the States were an established fact.

"There are, of course, always certain serious questions to be taken into account when one contemplates a new and final movement. Let me say, even in the changing of a house there are difficulties to be considered, and how much more so in the changing of a country. No doubt one of the gravest considerations among your friends must be that of labor. But then firstly, I think they ought to recollect that they are leaving a very difficult question of labor behind! They are not proposing to adopt São Paulo (I shall only talk of São Paulo) from any theory of colonization, leaving their old country in its old established perfection of labor and production; but they are leaving it from deep and weighty reasons which essentially arise from causes connected with the labor question there; they are leaving it because (among other painful features of the case) the former life of employer and laborer appears to them to be no longer possible! In contemplating, therefore, the difficulties of the labor question here, they must strictly bear in mind the difficulties of the labor question there: and that the comparison is not between the old and the new, but it is between the old, broken up and gone, with all its rough and wounding fragments lying abroad, and the new which has to be entirely built up, on open ground.

"Bearing all this in mind, so as to keep a proper estimate of the two positions well in sight, I do not think your friends need be very distrustful of the labor question here. We know it is a serious question and that there is lack of labor as a general rule, but then, as I have already told you in our conversations, and I think you allowed the justice of the observation, I believe the want of the regular laborer here to arise in a great degree from the want of the regular employer, and the regular pay for labor. Without employment we well know there cannot be a labor market, and hitherto in the agriculture of this province, there never has been regular employment offering remuneration. Hence the total absence of any working system.

"Now, on our own railway, we cannot truly say that we have ever felt the want of labor: yet when we first began, there certainly was an indisposition generally speaking to work. But bye and bye when one and the other found out that a week's labor really meant a week's money, and that the work was really there, and the constant master there too to pay the money for the work, then the laborer began to comprehend his real position better.

"One told the other how the case was, how the remuneration for his toil really glittered in his hand, on pay-day, and how he really earned his bread and independence; and very soon disinclination gave place to willingness, and all wanted to come and learn to work, and get their money as their friends were doing.

"Now once establish a good fixed employing class, such as a good army of your cotton-growers would be, and you will quickly have a good fixed laboring class. I speak even of the Province as it is: but see what changes are about to take place, and see what fame in Europe, a good settlement of your countrymen would spread! What changes, too, your own coming would of itself produce, with all your well-understood economy and machinery. Then, as I say in my letter, what a number of hands, hard-working hands on bad roads, our own railway and its expected feeders and branches, when open would set at liberty to work as you would teach them: consider, too, how your coming would expedite the road-making, and lastly what thousands of hard-working Germans would come to you from abroad: really hard-workers, ready and anxious to learn to employ themselves.

"These poor people have, already, from time to time, come over in crowds to Brazil: but they have been disappointed and disheartened, and of late the Brazilian emigration agents have been in great disrepute. I can give one good and very good reason for all this: viz., that on their arrival here, they have found no real community of employers, and that their scene of poverty was only changed from one country to another! These immigrants or colonists have thus done very little, either for themselves or for Brazil, and under a continuance of the present state of things, are, on both accounts, better away.

"But once established a good paying and employing community, such as your planters would be, then these poor industrious people would flock to Brazil again, and gaining a handsome living here, would be the very hands your people could best turn to account, and greatly benefit both themselves and Brazil!—I do not really fear the labor question; let your people only come, and they will draw the labor after them.

"Before making my letter too long, it occurs to me to say, too, that I think there is some fallacy in your friends all wishing to go so far up country. It is there, no doubt, that all the very richest lands lie, but then it is equally true that, as regards cotton, even where I accompanied my fellow-travellers, only seventeen leagues from this city, they found rough cultivation (as I have written) producing twice and three times their usual home qualities! Finding lands then, at less prices perhaps, why go away so far?—For coffee, I admit, this is necessary, but not for cotton. Even in the close neighborhood of this city, there are excellent lands for this cultivation. And on this particular point let me call your and their especial attention to the fact that the small sample which I first sent home to England in April, 1861, which began all this late movement of the last five years, (which I alone have fostered and promoted as a foreigner here) was gathered on ground, abandoned for years, on the margin of the River Tieté, not one league from where I am now writing! And that sample, rude and ugly as it was, was valued at a milreis or 50 cts. per lb! It was that extraordinary intelligence that set me to work here! Indeed let me further say, that an immense proportion of our present first real harvest of cotton, is grown on grounds in easy distance of the railway and São Paulo city. Nor is it only in the direction of our line that cotton grows.

"In the north of the Province, towards that of Rio de Janeiro, for example, there have been new plantations made, which this year, must give abundantly; and I speak of this fact emphatically, because the Government have just conceded the right to make a branch line to these districts, from our station at Rio Grande, which, you know, will bring them within three hours of the port of Santos. If such lands will give two and three times what lands in your States will give, for the reason set forth in my letter, what more can be desired, if only for a beginning? This whole Province, in proper hands, may, in a short time be made a garden of coffee, cotton, corn and sugar.

"Well! I will say no more, but I believe that you will not contradict anything that I have said.

You have paid us a short visit, and you made the best of your time while you were among us. Your countrymen have, many of them, now explored many distant parts, and all the information they have gathered will go home, written in truth, and speaking of things as they really found them. I cannot believe but that the result must be most happy for this Province in bringing to it a large proportion of those of your people who resolve to change their country. This will be to them a new one, full of speedy promise, and suffering only those drawbacks,—want of roads and houses,—which admit of easiest remedy.

"The form and figure exist, and only wait the drapery. The power is here and only wants the mover. Wherever your people tread, they will be able to draw produce from a ready and abundant soil, and settle almost where they will, it will respond with gratitude. Let them come and see

"The world is all before them, were to choose
"A place of rest, and Providence their guide!

"Believe me, my dear Sir,
"Very faithfully yours,
"T. T. Aubertin.

"Sao Paulo, *Feb.* 8, 1866."

CHAPTER XIV.

COTTON IN BRAZIL.

This chapter is taken from an editorial in the Anglo-Brazilian Times, of January 8, 1866:

Only three or four years ago, when the great North-American struggle was developing itself, and the minds of all persons interested in the absorbing question of the day—the future supply of that cotton on which so much of England's manufacturing supremacy was based, were eagerly exploring all the known countries of the world, in quest of new cotton-growing regions, whence to derive present supplies and render the manufacturers released from their almost total dependence upon a rival country,—in oracling upon the subject the general conclusion of writers on the cotton future, was, that India, is the only country possessing sufficient extent of cotton-growing districts to be practically a competitor with the Southern States for the possession of the markets of Europe: Brazil being summarily classed among the minor cotton regions, and cursorily set down as capable of furnishing perhaps two hundred thousand or three hundred thousand bales.

Yet, though it was not altogether unknown that cotton of a fine quality was indigenous in many parts, and furnished the Indians with several articles useful to them in their rude life; due attention was not paid to the circumstance of it being found so commonly disseminated in Brazil, nor to the fact that, in the days of gold and diamond mining, and seclusion from-free commercial intercourse, many small manufactories of coarse cotton cloths were located here and there, even in the scantily populated regions of Matto Grosso and Goyaz; some of which still exist, which supplied the unsybaritic wants of the Brazilians of those days, before the cheapening of the imported article, the greater luxury of tastes induced by more extended acquaintance with European wares, and the great demand for Brazilian products, turned attention from manufacturing pursuits and gold washings to the agriculture of the country as the most rapid means of acquiring wealth.

Now, however, through the increased importance which its culture assumed in the eyes of the Brazilian fazendeiros; in view of the high prices obtainable in the marts of Europe, prompted and encouraged by enlightened gentlemen, both native and foreign, who saw in the growth of cotton a source of emolument and prestige to Brazil, juster ideas can be formed of its capacities as a cotton-growing country. Under all these influences its culture has been revived in some localities, widely extended in others, essayed and found lucrative in many before unthought of, and not a province, save perhaps war-troubled Matto Grosso, but contributed to the largely increased exportation during the past year to the markets of Europe; and it can now be rested on as an established fact that, from the region directly under the equatorial sun to the southernmost and therefore coolest provinces; from the low lands bathed by the waters of the South Atlantic to the high plains of the west,—in almost the totality of the three millions of square miles comprised in the superficies of Brazil, the culture of cotton may be successfully pursued; and more—that the climate is so eminently favorable to its growth and harvesting that, were Brazil as practised as the United States in the employment of labor-saving implements and means of conveyance, such is its superiority in the quality and yield of herbaceous cotton as compared with the growth in the best cotton districts of the latter country that Brazil could afford to undersell the producers of the Southern States even in their own home ports.

Some of the cotton exported during the past year was gathered a thousand miles away in the interior, was freed from its seeds by the slow and costly operations of the antiquated churka gin, and was transported on mule back on a journey two months of steady travel, yet a price of some 12d a pound in Rio was sufficient to induce the farmers of that region to gather it from the cotton trees that grew around uncared for, and to submit it to the slow process of their inefficient and primitive cleaning machinery.

The culture of coffee has for many years been the favorite branch of Brazilian agriculture, giving enormous profits under a system of hoe labor and rapid exhaustion of the soil; but it is the opinion of many experienced men that, with the general employment of modern implements of husbandry and of improved gins for separating the fibre from the seed, cotton would rapidly surpass coffee on all lands adapted to the use of such implements; that when the labor of the negroes is supplemented by that of animals of traction, and the work and intelligence of one man thus represent the brute force alone of five or six under the present mode, the profits derived from the culture of the herbaceous annual, cotton, will be greater and surer than from the perennial, coffee. For the demonstrating of this proposition we look to the labors of the American planters now coming into Brazil, rather than to Brazilian fazendeiros, who, mostly used to a system of hand labor under which large profits are attainable, are not, as a body, prepared to give up old habits and prepossessions without having the demonstration wrought out before them.

But with this in sight; with the plow and the harrow in the field, staying exhaustion, increasing the yield and, besides, the breadth of land in cultivation; with improved cotton gins saving time and labor; with wagons on the farms and roads, facilitating and cheapening transport; it may reasonably be expected that, even with the present number of producing hands in Brazil, the export of cotton could be enormously increased without trenching on the production of coffee on its present scale.

Cotton, moreover, is a staple which is well adapted to the capabilities of white labor and small proprietorship. Its cultivation and gathering exact no excessive toil, or exposure to injurious influences. Children and women can assist in planting and harvesting without tasking their powers too strongly. The presses are a matter of home manufacture, and the outlay for a gin could be distributed among several individuals of the same settlement. And, what is of prime importance to this class, in selling the ligneous fibre of the cotton plant they do not send away the most valuable constituents of the soil, and therefore do not need, like the coffee planters, to maintain large tracts of virgin soil to substitute for their rapidly exhausting fields.

To the extended culture of this crop valuable results of a social order may arise. The great fazendeiro will not find it then his interest to extinguish the small proprietors to obtain new soil, nor to hold huge tracts of wild lands such as obstruct the march of improvement about Rio de Janeiro and in all the most accessible points. The interior districts, unsuitable to coffee, can be reclaimed from wildness, or the pasturage of a few thousand cattle, for the cultivation of a crop bearing the cost of transport; the colonies, borne down by their poverty, and the inability of their bulky productions to bear excessive freights, may take fresh root and thrive. The half vegetating poor Brazilian, now living miserably in some puny roça in the woods, little better than a slave of his rich and influential neighor, or following the three parts savage life ot a "troupeiro," may settle in the government colonies and become a freeman and a producer of wealth; the industrious Portuguese that carry their earnings and their labor home again, may be induced to devote these earnings to a profitable culture, and form homes for themselves; and agricultural immigrants will find in it that desideratum of the class, the means of procuring money with the annual first-fruits of their labor.

Cotton has a two-fold value in the eyes of the Political Economist. Not merely does its growth support and remunerate the agricultural producer, but its manufacture gives employment to many hands and many trades, stimulates many sciences, calls into action the powers of many minds, and brings wealth and comforts to all—and, if we cannot yield it the place of king of all the world, it cannot be denied that it has proved one of the mightiest engines of modern progress.

CHAPTER XV.

REPORT OF MAJ. ROBERT MERRIWETHER AND DR. H. A. SHAW TO MAJ. JOS. ABNEY, PRESIDENT SOUTHERN COLONIZATION SOCIETY, EDGEFIELD COURT HOUSE, S. C.

"SIR: In obedience to written instructions received from you, to examine portions of the Empire of Brazil, and report to you the result of our investigations, as to climate, productions, laws, religion, &c., we left Augusta, Ga., about the 18th of October, 1865, on the R. R., via Washington City, where we procured passports, and proceeded to New York. Securing passage on the "North America," one of the Brazil and United States line of steamers to Rio de Janeiro, we left New York on the 30th of October, and arrived at Rio de Janeiro on the 26th of November. Here we met several gentlemen from the South, who had been in Brazil several months, on the same mission that carried us thither. Amongst them we formed the acquaintance of Dr. GASTON, of Columbia, S. C., who had made rather an extensive tour in the interior of the province of St. Paulo. He introduced us to his Excellency, Paula Souza, Minister of Agriculture, to whom we explained the objects of our visit, and presented our credentials. The Minister offered us every facility desired in the prosecution of our investigations, furnishing transportation, a guide, an interpreter, and in most cases, food and lodging.

"The portions of the Empire we were instructed to visit and examine, were so extensive, and so difficult of access, with the means of transportation attainable in Brazil, that more than two years would have been required for the accomplishment of such an enterprise. We therefore concluded to select a portion of the Territory designated in our instructions, which we supposed best adapted to the wants and necessities of our people at home, and to confine our examinations to that particular Province.

"On our voyage out, we stopped at Pernambuco, where we satisfied ourselves that the climate would not suit the people of our State. It lies within ten degrees of the equator, and perpetual Summer reigns there. The climate is damp and hot, though said to be healthy, but yet the everlasting heat must enervate the system and break the constitution of man. In this province, however, is grown the best quality of upland cotton. Extracts from an English paper now at hand, quote Pernambuco cotton at from 1 to 1½d higher than any other in the great cotton mart of the world. Sugar and tobacco are also grown here in great perfection. We stopped also at Bahia, two or three hundred miles south of Pernambuco, where also cotton, sugar, tobacco and all the tropical fruits are grown in great perfection. Still, the climate, as in Pernambuco, is Equatorial, and liable to the same objections.

"After full and complete inquiry and investigation, the Province of San Paulo, lying between 22 and 25 degrees south latitude, appeared to us the most suitable for our people, on account of health, climate and productions, being by its whole length and breadth, just within the frost line, except its higher table lands, which are free from frost the year round. With the purpose of exploring this Province thoroughly, we left Rio de Janeiro, in company with Dr. Gaston, who, as above stated, had seen a considerable portion thereof, with the guide and interpreter, whom the Minister of Agriculture had commissioned to attend us, and went by steamer to Santos, its seaport town. We examined the country around this place, for fifty miles, but were not satisfied with its healthfulness, productions, or soil.

"Convincing ourselves that the country, lying between the mountains and seacoast, had no large bodies of farming lands, we directed our attention to the interior, beyond the mountains which bound the coast. Therefore, we took the cars over the San Paulo and Santos Railroad, the proprietors kindly giving us free passage both going and returning. This Railroad is not yet completed, but the cars pass over it to about twenty miles beyond the city of San Paulo, the capital of the province of the same name, and it is graded to Jundathy, forty miles from the capital. Its whole completed length is eighty or ninety miles, connecting the interior of the province with the seaboard, at Santos. This port, we omitted to mention, has a very capacious harbor, an inlet for ships of the largest class, and by the first of June, it is thought, its Railroad will be finished. A survey has been made to continue it about one hundred miles farther to Rio Clara, but no portion of it is under contract, and gentlemen conversant with its affairs, imagine some time will elapse before operations to extend it will commence.

"At San Paulo we were provided with animals to prosecute our journey over a country almost without roads; for the entire transportation in the interior is done on pack mules, except that now and then a bullock-cart is seen hauling at short distances, over roads which our wagons certainly could not pass. Those carts are of the most primitive character, the wheels and axles are fastened together, and all turn together in moving. We have often seen as many as ten oxen drawing at one cart, and sometimes many more, and not carrying more than two thousand pounds. The oxen, too, are as fine as we have ever seen.

"The traveller, in going from San Paulo to Botucatú, with the exception of these twenty or more miles of good farming lands, and a patch of woodland now and then, on which are usually a house and a small field, planted in corn and beans, will say he has travelled over a vast plain unfriendly to agriculture; and so, in our opinion, it is. But in the midst of this extensive campo or plain, or if you please, barren waste, suddenly rises up a mountain or succession of mountains, about fifty or sixty miles in length, by ten or twelve miles wide, evidently of a peculiar volcanic formation. As this mountain district was the most interesting visited, we examined it with the greatest care, and satisfied ourselves that it contained the richest lands we had ever seen. This immense and inconceivably fertile tract is owned, and, to some extent, cultivated by small farmers. Ask a man 'How much land do you own?' and his usual reply is, 'I do not know exactly, but it is four, six, or ten miles long, and from four to six miles broad.' The lands of Brazil, except in rare instances, have not been surveyed, and no one with whom we have conversed on this subject, knows how much land he owns; all guess. We saw corn growing on these lands, which would yield more than fifty bushels per acre. The timber is cut down, allowed to lie and dry for two months, commonly, and then set on fire. All the timber not consumed by the fire, remains just as the fire left it, till it rots. Then usually with a stick—sharpened at the end, sometimes with a hoe—a hole is made in the ground, the seed, from five to ten grains, put into this hole and covered with the foot, and this is all the cultivation the crops receive. Corn, cotton, rice, sugar cane, tobacco, coffee, and all the tropical fruits grow here in great perfection. We saw peaches and grapes also of good quality. The most of these lands are exempt from frost,—the health of this region is said to be unexceptionable—the water of the purest freestone, and the water-power equal to any in the world. Stock of all kinds, hogs and cattle especially, are superior. The usual depth of soil is supposed to be thirteen feet, but it is known to be twenty or more in some places. If this tract of country had convenient and easy communication with the trade of the world, if there might be any to equal, there could certainly be none to surpass it. Its present outlet is by the railroad, one hundred and twenty-five miles to its terminus, and from eighty to one hundred miles by it to Santos. Another outlet may be opened for it across the Big Sierra alluded to above. In that direction, it is from eighty to one hundred miles to steamboat navigation on the Juquiá River.

"These lands can be purchased at from one to two dollars per acre, and some tracts or parcels with considerable improvements.

"If a large number of families from the States should settle here, we have been assured officially, that good roads will be opened up immediately; and it is practicable to connect this district by railroad with the San Paulo Railroad, or by railroad over the Big Sierra to the head of navigation.

"Running parallel with this mountain range is the river Tieté, and for about twenty miles distant, on either side of which are lands of the best quality, producing every description of crops, except coffee, in the greatest perfection and abundance. There were some fields of as good, if not better cotton than we ever saw before, and without doubt the best 'cultivated grass,' whole fields of which were from five to seven feet high, and eaten by the animals with the greatest avidity. There, too, we found corn good enough for any country. Fifty bushels per acre is a small estimate for it. Our information is, that for more than one hundred miles down this valley, the same quality of land continues. It belongs to private individuals, and can be bought at from fifty to seventy-five cts. per acre. It is proper to mention here, that the territory forty or fifty miles south of the mountain range above referred to, is in the hands of the Indians. The lands in this valley we believe to be as good for cotton as any in the United States. The ordinary estimate of this crop is from two to three thousand pounds, with but little cultivation. The character of the soil is what is usually called with us 'mulatto,' and its depth from eight inches to five feet. But a great objection to this exceedingly fertile valley is its liability to chills, which are sometimes malignant.

"In describing these lands more particularly, it is perhaps proper to remark that the mountains, though rising to a considerable height, have usually several long slopes almost level in ascending them, and the larger portion of them is level enough for cultivation. You go along a slope slightly ascending, for several miles, then up a steep ascent for a half mile or so, to another long slope almost level, and so on till you reach the summit, which is also a large level tract, from a half to two miles wide. This land is nearly all 'terra roccha,' of the first quality. The woods are apparently one immense canebrake, though the cane is much larger than that grown in the States, and called here 'bamboo.' Timber is abundant; including furniture wood of the finest grain, and that most suitable and required for ship-building.

"We have been particular in the description of these lands, for if a number of our people go to Brazil, the districts of Botucatú and Lencoes, and the adjoining lands of the Tieté River, constitute the section we advise them to examine. In our opinion, a splendid future awaits this portion of the province.

"We saw other good lands, but they were in a high state of cultivation, for Brazil, and could not be purchased for less than twenty-five, fifty, and a hundred dollars per acre, since they were planted in coffee. At Arraquarra, about two hundred miles from San Paulo, a tract of country,—a fazenda as it is called there,—is offered for sale, by Dr. Gavias, of San Paulo, containing from one hundred and forty to one hundred and eighty thousand acres of land, for one hundred and twenty-five thousand dollars, on a credit of ten or fifteen years, if desired. We examined this, and suppose that from fifteen to twenty-five thousand acres of it are of *good quality*, including some coffee lands, and would produce corn, sugar, &c., to perfection. A large portion of it is campo, but the best quality of campo we have seen in the province. The other is woodland, and will produce corn and cotton very well. The fifteen to twenty thousand acres of good land alluded to above is 'terra roccha' as the Brazilians term it, which means land of inexpressible richness and fertility. Upwards of two hundred of very fine cattle are included in this great bargain; and a dwelling-house, some outbuildings, and one hundred acres of cultivated land comprise the improvements on the place. Each of us has a map of this great private domain, and will furnish it to any one who desires it, with all the information we have in regard to its advantages.

"Lands which lie too low for coffee, are very little estimated by the Brazilians, and in the district of Campenas, within twenty or thirty miles of the railroad, are some very fine farms, of this description, with good improvements, which can be purchased for from two to five dollars per acre.

Much of these lands are 'terra roccha,' and all of them will produce corn, sugar cane and cotton, admirably. Two gentlemen from the States, one from Alabama, and the other from Louisiana, have already purchased and settled there.

"This report would be incomplete and unsatisfactory, if concluded without a statement of the prices, particularly for the necessaries of life. The cost then of clearing forest lands, according to the custom of the country, is from $1.50 to $2.00 per acre. Horses, domesticated, can be bought for from $20 to $40; unbroken, from $15 to $30; mares, from $5 to $10; jacks, from $50 to $100; pack mules, from $25 to $30; riding mules, from $40 to $80; unbroken, in lots, from $12 to $15; fat hogs weighing two hundred pounds each, from $5 to $8; breeders and pigs, in proportion; sheep from $1.50 to $3.00 inferior and scarce; goats, from $1 to $2; milk cows, in lots, from $8 to $10; single, $12 to $15; oxen fat, from $12 to $20; work oxen, from $30 to $40; corn usually from 50 to 75 cts. Beans are worth from $1 to $1.25 per bushel; rice from $2 to $3; coffee from 7 to 10 cts. per pound; leather from $3 to $5, per side; sugar from 6 to 8 cts.; rum from 25 to 30 cts. per gallon; banannas, limes and lemons from ¼ to ½ ct. each; oranges from

½ to 1 ct. each, and pine-apples abundant, when in season, from 1 to 2 cts. each.

"The above are the prices furnished us by citizens in the interior. In the larger towns, most of these products, particularly fruit, are much higher.

"Should ever our people be disposed to emigrate to Brazil, it is of the utmost importance that there should be a concert of action among them. If they contemplate going in any considerable numbers, preliminary arrangements should be made for shelter and subsistence, and all of them should settle within a reasonable distance of one another. If this important consideration is lost sight of, many will, it is feared, become dissatisfied for the want of proper association, neighbors, &c., and the result will be, that they will have to move to other American settlements, or be merged, in a short time, in the native element by which they will be surrounded. A few families, or a few dozen families can find ample subsistence and shelter in most of the settlements visited by us, but if more than these propose to settle far in the interior, at the same time, we would advise them in order to avoid disappointment and distress, to make ample preparation before doing so. Notwithstanding we utter these words of caution, the citizens assure us that they will have plenty to subsist a very large number of immigrants, and in some cases have offered, with that generosity peculiar to the first class of Brazilians, to divide half their subsistence with us, without compensation. This offer includes corn, sugar, coffee, rice, &c. Flour cannot be had in the interior, as there is no wheat grown in San Paulo, though we understand that at one time wheat was one of the principle articles of export from this province. We believe, from the character of the best lands, that it could be grown with perfect success.

"The Government allows all immigrants to introduce, for their own use, free of duty, all articles of prime necessity, such as tools of all kinds, wagons, gear, machinery, furniture, &c. This should not be forgotten by the emigrant, for in the interior you will find only the hoe, ax, bill-hook, and bullock cart, and they, except the hoe, of the rudest manufacture. Plows can be had only in the larger towns, and none have been seen by us that are suitable for the ordinary cultivation of the products of this country. *Seed of every variety, especially for the garden, should be carried in bottles, securely corked.* Clothing, shoes, hats, dry goods, &c., can be bought cheaper in Brazil than in the United States. Heavy shoes, for plantation use, however, are scarce in this market. They should be taken from the States, and also plow-gear of all descriptions, as well as cooking utensils. Perhaps it would be advisable for each family to provide themselves with a suitable cooking-stove, as they will find no chimneys in the interior, brick scarce and expensive, and stone not very abundant in the vicinity of the best lands.

"In conclusion, you will pardon us for indulging in some general observations, as to the truthful result of our experience. The vast domain of Brazil, contains the most fertile soil in the Universe, and more cheap lands to allure the emigrant than any other nation under the sun. For the supply of the millions that will soon be flocking to her shores, she abounds in the precious metals and costly gems, and in the most valuable products known to commerce. 'The cattle upon a thousand hills' are hers, and may be yours, and such cattle as man never beheld in any other clime. The earth yields almost spontaneously, the grain and fruit and vegetables, that most delight the palate and satisfy the wants of men. To gratify the sportsman, the woods are full of game, of deer, of wild hogs, and partridges and quails, and of the most delicate birds of every hue and of every description, whilst her innumerable rivers and water courses teem with fish of the greatest variety and the finest flavor. And if the people do not catch and eat, it is only because her other productions are so highly prized that they deem it wiser to devote their time to those, and to fish with 'silver hooks.' There is nothing that man needs or can fancy, which he may not raise or procure here, with the least imaginable toil. Her water power is sufficient to drive all the machinery in the world, and her natural and material resources are equal to the support of the population of China.

"Below Rio de Janeiro, the seasons are precisely opposed to ours, their spring or planting season, beginning with the beginning of our Fall, and their summer beginning with our first, and ending with our last winter month. But that nothing may be wanting for the encouragement of the agriculturist, in this happy region, unlike most of the other portions of the habitable Globe, the summer is its wet, and the winter its dry season, and its good lands never wash away.

"It may be asked, however, what are the hindrances and drawbacks to the population and development of this wondrous territory? What natural enemies has it to man, and to the products of the earth? what wild ferocious animals, and enormous reptiles to disturb his repose, and what noxious insects to destroy the fruits of his labor? When we answer these questions frankly, you will be amazed at the hallucinations under which you have labored all your life. We traversed one Province for over a thousand miles, taking six months from our departure hence, to make our explorations, and during the whole of that period, we discovered no ravenous beasts worth naming, and only three or four serpents of diminutive size, and no more to be feared than those seen every day in your fields and forests. The insects that prey upon the crops, including the red ant, are not so destructive as those which infest our richest lands, and there is no rust or sufficient frost to check or obstruct the growth of their beautiful cotton. Moreover, since the memory of man, there has been no earthquake there, no subterranean fire, no volcanic eruptions to appal the hearts or to disturb the security of its inhabitants, and its men and women live to a riper old age than even in this once favored country.

"Though there are a few legal and religious or canonical impediments to the foreigner or emigrant, such as that he may not reach one or two of the highest offices in the State, and may not, if a Protestant, erect a Cross upon his Church, yet the whole spirit of Brazil is opposed to such hindrances, and a mighty and united effort is now being made, with the most certain prospects of success, to place the naturalized citizen and the native Brazilian on an exact equality, in all rights, in all privileges, and in all honors that the Government can bestow.

"The constitution of the Empire is modelled after the British, abating some of the most objectionable features, such as the rights of primogeniture, and a hereditary nobility, and the working of the government is harmonious, steady, just and powerful. The Emperor is a wise and magnanimous Ruler, sprung from an intellectual and illustrious race, and ready at all times to condescend to any man or thing, compatible with the dignity of his crown, for the advancement of the interests and the glory of his country. He and his ministry, and indeed, his entire people, appear to be animated and actuated by the same enlarged and generous views of the future greatness and the destiny of his wide and magnificent realm. The foreigner on entering his dominions finds no prejudices to combat, no antipathies to avoid, but a liberal Minister ready to welcome, and a population to greet him, and a Sovereign to offer him the powerful protection of his government.

"A large society for the promotion of emigration has been organized, and some of the ablest and most honored personages in the country appointed its directors. Its special objects are to aid and take care of the foreigner on his landing, to protect him from want as well as from the frauds of the designing, and to vindicate his rights and privileges before the Government and the councils of the nation. The Government has also established a Hotel for the shelter and accommodation of the same class of individuals. Corps of engineers and surveyors have been appointed to open roads and survey lands, and there is a spontaneous movement of the whole Empire to open wide its arms for the men of enterprise and labor of all nations who have a mind to seek the grandest theatre for the exercise of their energies and the display of their genius ever presented on the face of the green earth.

"Very respectfully,

"Your obedient servants,

"Robert Merriwether,

"H. A. Shaw."

CHAPTER XVI.

(CONDENSED, FROM A LITTLE WORK ON BRAZIL, BY WILLIAM SCULLY.)

A TRAVELLER without a guide-book, is like a ship at sea without a compass; and must resign himself to being dragged about in the wake of a courier who, though perhaps long a resident, may yet remain perfectly ignorant of the manners and customs of the people, and of the points of interest in the country.

A man must carry knowledge with him, if he desires to bring more home; but it is a lamentable fact that many persons leave Brazil, after a long residence in it, as ignorant of its grand sights, and of the laws, institutions, and habits of the people, as when they came; remaining, as is too often the case, prejudiced against what they had not even tried to understand.

One great requisite in a traveller is coolness of

temper. Contrarieties will arise even in the best organised countries; and, in Brazil, where *espere um pouco* (wait a little), *ámantiã* (to-morrow), and *paciencia* (patience), are words in every one's mouth, an easy-tempered man makes the best traveller. Therefore let your motto be "keep cool;" and if circumstances absolutely require the *fortiter in re*, at least let it be tempered with the *suaviter in modo;* for the Brazilian is innately courteous, and, appreciating in a high degree the quality in others, will yield much more to the politeness and suavity of the stranger than could be extorted by the menaces of the Foreign Office.

Passports are necessary, and may be procured either from the Brazilian consuls, or from the authorities of your own country, but we recommend the latter in every case. The different members and the servants of a family can travel with the one passport if they be included in it. On arrival, it will be viséd at once by the police officer, and handed back to you on board. On wishing to leave Brazil you will have to advertise your intention for three preceding days, or procure some respectable person to become responsible for your debts and liabilities.

Could the intelligent English, Irish, and Scotch agriculturists, possessed of small capital, be induced to scale the confining walls of home-ties and prepossessions, to come here to judge for themselves of the climate, the resources, and the capabilities of this vast and fertile empire, on which nature, in the collocation and accumulation of its mineral and agricultural wealth, seems to have smiled benignantly, and to have lavished with a munificent hand her choicest treasures, we think that few would be willing to leave the prospects which it offers to the enterprising and industrious farmer, whether in the pursuit of agriculture or of grazing—prospects far superior to those offered by Australia, New Zealand, or the United States.

It is too much the fashion with foreigners to make "odious comparisons" between Brazil and their own country. They may be perfectly conscientious in their belief, but, with the superficial knowledge they acquire without mingling with the natives, they become discontented, knowing nothing of the real kindness, courtesy, and hospitality of the people among whom they may be mere "birds of passage;" and in their writings and conversation the temptation of a well-rounded period, or pointed sarcasm, often carries the day against their better sense of justice.

To no citizen of any country is it becoming to play the Pharisee, for in no country are the institutions and customs beyond improvement, or beyond criticism and detraction.

The constitution and the laws of Brazil are a reflex of the English. The Emperor is a highly educated gentleman, speaking most European languages; and as a monarch, is a pattern to those of Europe. The Empress is a lady, and a Christian, and she and her illustrious husband are easy of access alike to rich and poor.

The court and aristocracy of Brazil have learnt to carry their pride without offence, and there is a rising class which is rearing imperishable monuments of their zeal and patriotism in the promotion of just and salutary laws. Religious opinions of all kinds are respected, and though a Roman Catholic country, the Government pays Protestant clergymen for the benefit of the German colonists.

The River Plate is a nest of petty republics constantly at cross purposes, and without any combined plan of material progress; Monte Vidéo, a State bankrupt in everything but oppression; and the other republics of South America, smouldering volcanoes, ready at any moment to vomit forth anarchy and bloodshed.

Foreigners are welcomed into Brazil, and the people and Government endeavor by every means to encourage emigration; and, with the great facilities afforded, and the immense field for enterprise for industrious agriculturists, it is surprising that Scotch and Irish emigrants do not seek this country, where a life of more prosperity and of greater ease awaits them than can be realised in the United States, where the foreigner is despised, and where the frightful winter of an arctic clime exacts from the planting farmer excessive labor in a summer heat that is never experienced even in the hottest equatorial regions of Brazil.

Brazil, in truth, enjoys the finest, the most equable, and the healthiest climate that is found in any country. Her soil yields everything that tropical and temperate climes produce; and, if there were but sufficient labor, she could easily become the source from which Europe would obtain, not only her luxuries and her comforts, not only the staples which feed her manufactures, the dyewoods, the indigo and the cochineal of her dyers, the drugs, gums, balsams, and resins of her druggists, but even the grain and cattle with which she nourishes her population.

THE IMPERIAL FAMILY.

The present Emperor, Dom Pedro II., ascended

the throne of Brazil while only five years old, his father, Dom Pedro I., having abdicated in his favor on April 7, 1831.

The ceremony of his coronation took place on July 18, 1841, and on September 4, 1843, he espoused the present Empress, Donna Theresa Christina Maria.

It is not too much to say that it is to the wise and vigorous administration of the present Emperor that Brazil owes her present rank among civilised nations, and the prosperity and tranquillity she has enjoyed for so many years, in the midst of the continuous outbreaks against law and order which have desolated, and ruined the unhappy republics that surround her. In achieving this great result the personal character and acquirements of the Emperor have been of incalculable service, as displaying a high standard of excellence, in manners, education, and morality, to which his courtiers and his people might aspire. Foremost and indefatigable in every project likely to advance the interests of his country, morally or materially, he has used the great powers entrusted to him by the Constitution, and the still greater acquired through the influence of his own character and talents, for the benefit of the people themselves, and not for the aggrandisement of himself or family, and it is no wonder that, imbibing his spirit and stimulated by his example, the public men of Brazil number among their ranks some of the most patriotic and large-minded statesmen to be found in the world.

His Majesty is accessible to all ranks of society, and ready to listen to any tale of distress. His annuity of 800,000 milreis ($400,000) scarcely enables him to obey the dictates of his heart in the distribution of his charity.

Nor in this beautiful characteristic is Her Majesty the Empress deficient; the 96,000 milreis she receives annually is chiefly disbursed, not in the wasteful extravagance of fashion, but in the alleviation of poverty and sickness, she contenting herself in her dress with the elegant simplicity of taste, without the ornamental jewellery and expensive modes of Paris.

The two princesses, one nineteen years, the other eighteen years old, have been very carefully educated by the most competent professors procurable, and under the personal superintendence of the Emperor, who, whatever his avocations, devoted an hour each day to their instruction in history and geography.

The eldest, Donna Isabel, is heiress to the throne, the Salic law not obtaining in Brazil; great expectations are entertained from her well-known amiable disposition and natural talent. She was married on October 15, 1864, to Louis Gaston d'Orleans, Compte d'Eu, a grandson of Louis Phillippe, who distinguished himself greatly while in the Spanish service during the last war between Spain and Morocco.

The younger sister, Donna Leopoldina, married Augustus, Duke of Saxe Coburg, a member of the richest and most illustrious family in Germany.

MANNERS AND CUSTOMS.

Among the various classes of which Brazilian society is composed, the nobility naturally claims the first attention. As the creation of a Brazilian aristocracy took place only after the declaration of Independence in 1822, the length of their pedigrees is not great, and by a very wise and salutary law, all titles conferred on persons becoming extinct at their death, so that, in order that their heirs may obtain the same honors, they must render some public service which will merit the appreciation of the Emperor, whose selection is in conformity with all his public acts. He confers "honor only on those to whom honor is due." The nobility possess many amiable qualities. They are temperate, generous, charitable, attached to their sovereign, and courteous to their inferiors in society. Even when occupying the offices of Ministers of State, the affable manner in which they receive both foreigner and native, contrasts very agreeably with the assumed dignity and inaccessibility of the English placeman.

This is truly a pleasant characteristic of Brazilian officials, from the highest to the lowest; and even the Emperor, at his levees, denies access to none, receives petitions, and listens courteously to any requests or communications made to him by native or foreigner, usually speaking the language of the latter. At the office of a Minister of State, the applicant of any degree enters in his turn, is bowed to a chair, and is received as if he were conferring a favor rather than seeking one. If he is a foreigner, his native tongue is used in preference; his views are listened to and discussed, and when he takes his leave it is with a feeling that, even if not adopted, they will, at least, receive a full consideration.

The ladies, in their out-door life, usually attire themselves in the latest Paris fashions, and, on days of ceremony and celebrations, don their finest dresses and most brilliant jewellery. At home, however, they in general are seen in very plain apparel, employed industriously in some small domestic economy.

Many of the ladies are very attractive in their appearance and in their manners. Among them you cannot find the blue-stocking or the strong-minded lady, for in literary pursuits the Brazilian ladies are content to be modest.

The Brazilian gentlemen are remarkable for temperance and frugality, and for natural talent may compete with any other nation, but so much cannot be said of their industry. Some yield themselves up to the charms of literature and science, but most of the upper class are content with a monotonous daily round of existence, made up of many naps during the day, gapes over the balconies in the afternoon, and a réunion in the evening, with an occasional visit to the opera.

The Brazilians show much courtesy and kindness to strangers who come among them; and it is by no means a rare thing for them to voluntarily take a great deal of trouble to do them a service. In their intercourse with one another they are very sociable, but somewhat ceremonious. Even among the working-classes and the blacks, two acquaintances never meet in the street without an interchange of compliments. A negro, doffing his hat, addresses his friend with—"*Salveo Deos,*" or "*Deos the dê bons dias;*" then follows a full inquiry into the state of his health, and that of his family and relations; and on parting the compliments are regularly renewed. It is also the custom among Brazilians, when speaking to one another, to remove their hats, and to remain uncovered until desired to put them on.

In their receptions, whenever a stranger comes in, he is immediately saluted by every one present; and, if seated, they all rise to pay him respect. When receiving a visitor, the master of the house is not too proud to go to the door to meet him, with the most affable expression of—"*Tenha a bondade d'entrar, a casa é sua,*" and ushers him into the room, himself following behind. On leaving the room, the order is reversed, and the host then precedes his guest. The parting ceremony usually begins at the top of the stairs, and consists ordinarily of an "*Adeos*" accompanied with a bow; the guest then descends a few steps, followed by the host; here take place a few more complimentary exchanges; and finally, at the door, the guest again turns round and salutes his friend, and a few more bows and polite expressions pass between them. On meetings, however, of more than ordinary interest—such as that of long absent friends—their mutual sympathy expresses itself in a warm and hearty embrace; one lifting the other fairly off the ground—a welcome rather embarrassing to an Englishman when first subjected to it. The salutations of ladies among themselves, both at meeting and parting, are not less ardent and affectionate; and are made on all occasions by a mutual profusion of kisses on both cheeks.

HISTORY.

Brazil was first discovered on April 22, 1500, by Pedro Alvares Cabràl, who landing at Porto Seguro, took possession of the country in the name of the Portuguese king, Dom Manoel, in the reign of whose successor, Dom João III., the country was granted to twelve donatorios for the purpose of colonisation; they, however, being able to effect little, the grants finally reverted to the Crown, either by purchase or resumption. The Indian population, consisting of one hundred and sixty tribes, offered great obstacles to the settlement, and during the absorption of Portugal by Spain, the Dutch possessed themselves, from 1624 to 1654, of the sea-coast provinces from the Maranhão to the S. Francisco. The immigration of the Portuguese Court, during the seizure of Portugal by Napoleon, gave a great impulse to the development of the country, but after the return of the King to Portugal, the dissatisfaction of the Brazilians at their connexion with Portugal led, on September 7, 1822, to the proclamation of their independence, and Dom Pedro I., the son of the King of Portugal, was declared the first Emperor of Brazil; he granting the present Constitution enjoyed by the people. However, April 7, 1831, this monarch abdicated in favor of the now reigning Emperor, Dom Pedro II., under whom Brazil has settled down into its present state of peace and prosperity.

The *mineral* wealth of Brazil is extraordinarily great, but remains undeveloped from want of capital, enterprise, and labor, almost the only receipts being from the gold and diamond washings, which, after yielding two tons of diamonds and eight hundred of gold, seem exhausted of their rich stores, and have been in a great measure abandoned. Most of the known metals and precious stones have been found, and iron, the most useful of all, is in great abundance throughout. Coal is in a degree deficient, for though immense deposits of lignite and valuable bituminous earth exist in the central provinces, true coal has been found only in those at the extreme south.

EMIGRATION.

The attention of emigrants has not hitherto been directed to Brazil, although this country possesses many advantages over others to which a continuous stream of emigration is pouring.

In the main, the chief reason for this is, undoubtedly, the want of precise knowledge of the country, as the books hitherto published have been devoted more especially to those striking characteristics in the geology, vegetation, animal life, and peculiarities of the country generally, which were of a nature to interest and amuse the reading public, but which served little purpose towards affording the *emigrant* the *practical* information which he needs.

Another reason is, the most erroneous idea which prevails respecting the Brazilian climate—that it is unhealthy. Far from this; it can rank with the healthiest and most *enjoyable* climates of the world.

Brazil contains about 1,900,000,000 acres of land, upon which is a population of about 9,000,000 This, however, is not equally distributed.

In the whole of the immense valley of the Amazonas in the north, comprising one-third of the whole extent of Brazil, there is a population of only 100,000. In the interior a similar disproportion exists, and nine-tenths of the free population, and almost all the slaves, are gathered into the strip of low land along the sea-coast where sugar, cotton, and tobacco are cultivated, and particularly into the province of Rio de Janeiro and the other coffee-growing districts around it, the remainder of the country being abandoned to solitude, to the working of such gold washings as still repay the rude processes used, and to the rearing of cattle and horses.

The level valley of the Amazon, and the low land along the coast, constitute the hot region of Brazil.

South of the valley of the Amazon and east of the low land of the coast, is a vast elevated region buttressed up as it were on hills and mountains.

This high land rises somewhat rapidly in the north; towards the east lifts itself abruptly out of the low land; in the middle attains its greatest elevation among the mountains of Minas Geraes, which turn into great plains and low swells as they recede westward into Goyaz and Matto Grosso; and in the south falls, and approaches nearer to the sea until the high land and the mountains on the sea-coast die away into the low mountains, hills, and plains of the province of Rio Grande do Sul.

Two important effects result from this elevation

of the interior, of which the first is that, though many large navigable rivers enter this high land, falls occur where their descent is made into the low land, which prevent continuous navigation from and to the sea, and thus it is only in the south-western part of Matto Grosso and in the southern province of Rio Grande do Sul (otherwise S. Pedro do Sul) that a free interior communication with the sea exists—with Matto Grosso by the Paraguay through the Paraná, and with Rio Grande do Sul by the Uruguay, this and the Parana joining near Buenos Ayres to form the river Plate.

The other effect is, that the elevation of the land added to the direction of the wind diminishes the temperature so much as to render even the most northern part moderate in its heat, while in the southern half slight frosts occur in winter, and the climate is moderate and pleasant.

The climate, therefore, of all this vast region fits it for the residence of Europeans, and all the crops usually cultivated in Europe may be grown on it, including tobacco, cotton, Indian corn (maize) and wheat, besides tea, mandioca, coffee in the warmer parts, and a host of other tropical plants, while it is likewise well suited to the rearing of cattle, horses, mules, goats, and sheep.

In the northern half, however, the seasons are

too regularly divided into the wet and dry, and great droughts are so common and injurious as to unfit a large proportion of it for an agricultural region without resort to irrigation; and, as in Buenos Ayres, at times the cattle even die from want of water in localities.

In the southern half the seasons are not injuriously regular, and rains fall more or less throughout the year; this region, therefore, is well fitted in all respects for both agriculture and grazing.

The great valley of the Amazon (including the provinces of Pará and Amazonas) is suitable to the cultivator of sugar, tobacco, cotton, cocoa, and a thousand other natives of warm countries; and from this valley comes the gum-elastic and a great deal of the sarsaparilla of commerce. Cattle also can be raised, but not sheep, as the climate is too damp and warm for these last.

Along the sea-coast low land the cultivated products are similar, and coffee is raised upon its cooler and drier slopes. The same remarks apply respecting sheep, and both regions are covered with timber, unless where it has been cleared for the cultivation of the land.

On the northern half of the interior, highland sheep and cattle thrive, and must be the main dependence, particularly sheep, which require less water comparatively than cattle. In the southern half lies, therefore, the best field for such emigrants as do not purpose to cultivate sugar-cane and perennial tropical plants. In this interior country, and particularly in the province of Rio Grande do Sul, the mountains and the banks of streams are timbered, but plains form a feature and afford excellent pasture and agricultural land, similar to the prairies of the United States, and the River Plate.

The great drawback in Brazil is the scarcity of roads for vehicles, and, indeed, of good roads of any kind. This want was not so much felt, as the lands in cultivation lie usually at no great distance from the sea, but the disadvantages arising from their absence have been so strongly impressed upon the Government and people in the present war, by the difficulties encountered in forwarding troops and supplies overland, that we believe a great change is commencing in this respect, and that many good roads will be established between all the main points at least, thus opening up vast tracts of splendid country to settlements; still, our advice would be to wool-raisers, not to withdraw far from roads, and to agriculturists, to settle only in their vicinity, since ready access to a market is the greatest advantage they can have, particularly in a country where transport of produce is high.

Besides the rivers, there are five railways which go towards the interior. The northernmost, belonging chiefly to an English company, starts from the port of Pernambuco, and runs for miles through a sugar and cotton raising country. The next, also in most part belonging to an English company, runs from the port of Bahia, through a country where sugar, cotton, and tobacco are the main productions. The third, originating at the port of Rio de Janeiro, the capital of the empire, opens out a fine coffee region, but has only a portion yet finished. The fourth starts from the vicinity of Rio de Janeiro, and, in connection with the splendid carriage road made by the União and Industria Company, develops an excellent coffee and agricultural district, and forms communication with the interior pastoral and agricultural province of Minas Geraes, whence is derived a large proportion of the food and exports of the capital. The fifth will be completed this year, and runs from the port of Santos in the province of S. Paulo, on to the high interior plains of that province, and will open out a large extent of coffee, agricultural and pastoral country. Another railway, projected by an English company, will start from the point of Rio Grande do Sul, and traverse perhaps the finest part of that splendid province to the vast coal-beds on the Candiota branch of the river

Jagunarão. The Government is pushing on the construction of a road bringing the interior of the province of Paraná in ready communication with its seaports.

The great tide of emigration to the Americas has been to the United States in North America, and Buenos Ayres in South America, yet Brazil possesses inherent advantages over both, especially for emigrants with enterprise and some capital.

As compared with the northern United States, the climate is incomparably more genial, and therefore life is easier both to the agriculturist and the grazier. In the one, frosts are rare and slight, pasture continues in the winter, and thus the labor of the farmer may be spread, as in England, over the whole year, and the grazier need not hoard by vast supplies of winter provender for his stock. In the other the soil is frost-bound for five to seven months, during which the plow is useless and the farmer's labor is crowded into six months of sweltering weather; the pasture is killed or covered up with snow, and the wintering of their animals dissipates the stores which the farmer gathered with so much toil and cost, and which, to feed out, required so much additional cost and labor.

In Brazil less expense is necessary in houses, clothes, bed-clothes, firing, shelter for cattle, &c.

Coffee, sugar, and beef, are very cheap; food is more easily grown, the preservation of vegetables is not endangered and made difficult by intense frosts, and not only can all that is grown in the United States be raised in Brazil, but the mildness of the winter allows of the cultivation of many valuable tropical plants, and gives great advantages in the cultivation of such commercial staples as cotton, coffee, and tobacco.

Other advantages exist in the small cost at which the emigrant can obtain his working beasts, horses and cattle being worth only from £1 to £2 (five to ten dollars).

It is a knowledge of the advantages which a mild climate offers to a settler which has of late years drawn a rapidly increasing emigration to the great treeless plains of Buenos Ayres, where stone, and wood for fencing and firing are almost unknown, and which makes the settlers content to burn thistles for cooking purposes and brick-making, and endure the chilliness of winter without a fire. Brazil, however, in the great expanse of country which we have indicated as the best field for emigration, possesses the advantages of a still more genial climate than Buenos Ayres, and is without its disadvantages; for stone is abundant, and timber sufficient for house and farming purposes is found upon the streams; and this Brazilian region is free from those periodic storms of wind and sleet which cause so much damage and loss to graziers, and also from the excessive droughts which render Buenos Ayres unfit for agriculture, and at times destroy cattle by thousands.

The Government of Brazil has been for a long time most desirous of drawing emigration to this country, and some years ago undertook to do this by the establishment of assisted colonies, and by encouragement and aid given to the provinces, and to companies and individuals to establish others. The colonies, however, have not been so successful as the sacrifices made by the Government should have warranted; for though some have done moderately well, others have stood still, and several have decayed.

Several influences and circumstances have operated towards this result. One is, that a large proportion of the emigrants introduced consisted of the floating scum of Continental Europe, penniless and worthless. They were located on heavy timber land, where the ground had to be cleared before any crops could be sown. The crops cultivated were such as required to be manufactured in some degree before being ready for market, and therefore required a certain amount of capital and skill, which the poor class of emigrants could not supply; the want of roads discouraging the growth of the more bulky crops for sale; the absence of a ready sale at home for the articles produced, owing to the want of capital and enterprise, and the diminutive quantity of production; the excessive rates of transport and freight to the place of export, that too greatly reduced the value of the products at the farm. Add to these, the inexperience, incapacity, or mismanagement on the part of the directors of the colonies, and, in the case of the private colonies, too often a want of due regard to the requirements and interests of the colonists, who were made subjects of speculation by the owners or their managers, and it cannot be a matter of surprise that so few of the colonies have succeeded, even to a moderate extent.

In our opinion, the greatest error was in locating such emigrants in a timbered country, for timber land means bad roads and wearying, excessive labor; and the mere clearing of a few acres for a crop burdened the colonist with an amount of debt which, in an open country, would have supplied him with the implements and stock necessary to a successful start.

It must be borne in mind that where the condition of the roads, or where the distance from the seaport makes transport costly or difficult, only such articles as are valuable in proportion to their weight and bulk are profitable to the farmer, and therefore wool-raising is best fitted to the circumstances of an interior settlement. But while he might depend upon his wool for his main income, the settler ought not to follow the lazy practice of the Buenos Ayrean, and even of the Brazilian graziers, who live on beef or mutton, guiltless of any variation of their meat with such things as bread, vegetables, milk and butter, purely from too great indolence to cultivate a plot of ground, or milk a cow, among the hundreds they may have around them.

Foreigners arriving in this country without a passport are allowed to land unless suspected of being malefactors. A certificate from their respective legation or consulate will stand substitute for that document in case of need.

Those who are provided with passports can reside wherever they please, and travel all over the empire by obtaining a "visto" on it, which is granted gratis by the police authority, when passing from one to another province.

Foreigners going abroad are bound, like the Brazilians themselves, to advertise for three successive days their intended departure, in the interest of their creditors.

The expense of a passport to go abroad amounts to about 12*s*. (three dollars).

A foreigner residing in the empire for two years, having an establishment, or known to be of good conduct, or if married to a Brazilian woman, can travel freely in the interior of the country, being provided with a certificate from the police authority proving any one of the said circumstances.

The residence in this country is not dependent upon any permit from a public authority.

Foreigners are only bound, like all Brazilians, by municipal law, and, for statistical purposes, to produce a list of the persons composing their families, on the occasion of occupying a house. Even this formality is seldom practised.

Foreigners enjoy all the civil rights of Brazilians; they can acquire and possess all sorts of property, and dispose of it in every way; exercise all branches of trade, commerce, and industry, wholesale and retail. All employments not considered public ones are accessible to them. Brokers, auctioneers, and dispatchers in the custom-houses are considered public employments, being in the gift of Government. Yet foreigners are allowed to clear goods at custom-houses, when their own or consigned to them.

Naturalized Brazilians enjoy all the rights of

natives, except that they cannot become Deputies or Ministers of State. All other public employments and situations are open to them.

Two years' residence and good conduct are the only conditions required by law for the naturalization of foreigners; but the Parliament is daily dispensing with the former condition in all applications from acceptable individuals.

Colonists arriving in this country enjoy special facilities for their settlement. An agency office for colonization was established here last year, where all information upon lands to be sold, and other particulars, can be easily obtained.

A steady monarchical representative government, now forty-two years old, guaranteeing individual liberty by an *Habeas Corpus* law exactly such as exists in England; general religious toleration; unfettered liberty of the press; trial by jury; free right of association and petition; no hereditary aristocracy or titles; no distinction of castes; perfect equality before the law; are the principal political features of the Brazilian nation.

Ships bringing emigrants enjoy certain advantages; and the extended commerce with the great seaports of Europe and the United States enable the emigrants to reach Rio de Janeiro with facility from London, Liverpool, Glasgow, Southampton,

Newcastle, Newport, Cardiff, Swansea, Sunderland, etc., in the United Kingdom; Bremen, Hamburg, Havre, Bordeaux, Marseilles, and the chief ports of the continent of Europe both in the north and south. From the United States a brisk intercourse is maintained through New York and Baltimore, Boston, Philadelphia, and probably soon again from New Orleans and other Southern ports. At Rio de Janeiro is a Government lodging-house for emigrants, where board is supplied at moderate rates. An officer is deputed to go on board each vessel and furnish information to the emigrants; and at the lodging-house, and the office of the Official Agent any required elucidation can likewise be obtained. Luggage, and agricultural implements, can be imported free of duty.

In the province of Paraná the Government holds a very large quantity of land. In the district of Assunguy, where is the Government colony of Assunguy, there are three townships surveyed, platted and laid off in sections and colonial lots. These are settling up, and therefore five other contiguous townships have been surveyed and are ready for subdivision. Next to these, in the direction of the province of S. Paulo, and towards Cananeâ and Iguape, two important ports of S. Paulo, there is a great extent of Government timber land and prairie, well adapted for a great immigration. All this immense region communicates on one side with the city of Coritiba, the capital of Paraná, and thence by the Graciosa road with the ports of Antonina and Paranaguá, situated on the Bay of Paranaguá, and a road could be run direct to the latter port; on the other side are the village of Castro and other important ones of the interior, whence come the supplies of cattle; and on another side with the province of S. Paulo, running down to the coast of Cananeâ and to the Ribeira de Iguape, whose waters take their rise in the districts of Assunguy.

COMMERCE OF BRAZIL.

THE FOLLOWING TABLES SHOW THE GROWTH OF THE COMMERCE OF THE EMPIRE IN TEN YEARS.—THIS, IT WILL BE SEEN, IS VERY SATISFACTORY.

IMPERIAL EXPORTS *for* 1862–'63 *compared with* '53–'54,

DESTINATION.	TOTAL, 1853–'54.	TOTAL, 1862–'63.
British Possessions	$12,451,715	$23,123,764
English Channel	....	7,992,862
French Possessions	3,055,073	7,723,261
Portuguese Possessions	1,671,043	3,851,413
United States	11,892,750	7,629,058
River Plate	1,632,937	2,576,144
Chile	393,460	480,526
Denmark	1,012,601	513,189
Belgium	683,969	521,877
Hanse Towns	3,178,463	2,525,385
Spain	323,039	1,182,073
Sweden	840,837	1,173,736
Russia	56,546	295,778
Sardinia	339,928	285,609
Austria	1,355,044	187,197
Turkey	58,121	183,334
Mediterranean	....	350,869
Mexico	....	67,900
For consumption	....	34,965
Holland	51,475	58,925
Africa	....	220,931
Ports not specified	424,245	261,197
TOTAL	$38,421,246	$61,239,975

and showing the Imports at each Port in 1862–'63.

Rio de Janeiro.	Bahia.	Pernambuco.
$4,597,101	$5,073,943	$2,006,993
6,090,911	....	627,326
5,166,760	487,411	493,307
867,483	732,436	931,872
4,848,019	235,679	638,699
805,964	241,848	754,536
42,590	....	225,533
456,367	....	....
472,749	....	....
704,388	1,592,135	....
110,227	91,855	518,559
956,756	180,865	36,114
295,779	....	....
169,628	99,153	....
187,198	....	....
183,334	....	....
350,869	....	....
67,900	....	....
31,332	....	2,845
....	58,422	104
....	220,932	....
....	....	....
$26,405,304	$9,046,679	$6,235,888

IMPERIAL EXPORTS *for* 1862–'63 *compared with* '53–'54,

DESTINATION.	MARANHAO.	PARÁ.
British Possessions......	$1,563,128	$964,857
English Channel.........	....	....
French Possessions.......	103,317	662,825
Portuguese Possessions...	565,925	288,316
United States...........	104,715	816,589
River Plate............	....	....
Chile	....	....
Denmark...............	....	....
Belgium	....	....
Hanse Towns...........	....	37,070
Spain.................	23,915	....
Sweden.....	....	....
Russia	....	....
Sardinia	....	16,878
Austria	....	....
Turkey................	....	....
Mediterranean	....	....
Mexico	....	....
For consumption........	....	....
Holland...............	....	399
Africa	....	....
Ports not specified.......	....	....
TOTAL........	$2,361,000	$2,786,934

and showing the Imports at each Port in 1862–'63 (cont.)

Rio Grande do Sul.	S. José do Norte.	Porto Alegre.	Uruguayana.
$690,947	$860,483	$870	....
....	....	....	....
216,979	39,942	....	....
225,129	10,028	....	....
583,144	1,939	....	....
97,595	4,805	101,748	$84,398
....	....	....	....
....	....	....	....
47,573	....	....	....
333	....	....	....
154,899	....	....	....
....	....	....	....
....	....	....	....
....	....	....	....
....	....	....	....
....	....	....	....
....	....	....	....
....	....	....	....
....	....	....	....
....	....	....	....
....	....	....	....
....	....	....	....
$2,016,599	$917,197	$102,618	$84,398

IMPERIAL EXPORTS *for* 1862–'63 *compared with* '53–'54,

DESTINATION.	SANTOS.	PARANAGUÁ.
British Possessions......	$3,239,343	....
English Channel.........	....	....
French Possessions.......	181,927	....
Portuguese Possessions...	153,348	....
United States...........	312,276	....
River Plate............	....	$338,511
Chile.................	....	198,434
Denmark...............	....	....
Belgium	....	....
Hanse Towns...........	190,332	....
Spain	128,472	....
For consumption........	788	....
Ports not specified......	....	....
TOTAL.........	$4,206,486	$536,945

DESTINATION.	ALAGOAS.	SERGIPE.
British Possessions......	$2,079,360	....
English Channel.........	237,717	433,944
French Possessions......	....	....
Portuguese Possessions...	17,704	59,169
River Plate............	19,758	3,254
Denmark...............	....	56,822
Spain..................	28,192	....
Ports not specified.......	....	....
TOTAL........	$2,382,731	$553,189

and showing the Imports at each Port in 1862–'63 (cont.)

Antonina.	Parahiba.	Ceará.	Santa Catharina.
....	$1,324,445	$622,190	$1,404
....	257,315	345,648	....
....	158,679	172,999	....
....	....	....	....
....	82,572	....	5,423
$78,422	....	....	45,303
13,969	....	....	....
....	....	....	....
....	....	....	1,554
....	....	1,129	....
....	125,956	....	....
....	....	....	....
....	....	....	....
$92,391	$1,948,967	$1,141,966	$53,684

Espirito Santo.	Rio Grande do Norte.	Piauhy.	Mato Grosso.
$26,264	....	$72,432	....
....	....	....	....
....	....	39,118	....
....	....	....	....
....	....	....	....
....	....	....	....
....	....	....	....
....	$ 236,304	....	$24,894
$26,264	$236,304	$111,550	$24,894

IMPERIAL EXPORTS *to*

WHENCE EXPORTED.	1857–'58.	1858–'59.
Rio de Janeiro..........	$22,210,804	$329
Bahia.................	6,709,806	25,987,298
Pernambuco............	7,129,634	7,732,792
Maranhão..............	1,385,313	7,002,983
Pará..................	1,774,816	1,227,052
Rio Grande do Sul......	1,647,346	1,958,689
S. José do Norte.........	584,511	2,077,400
Porto Alegre...........	28,833	617,600
Uruguayana..	147,523	43,865
Santos................	1,639,383	1,866,579
Paranaguá.............	949,009	537,081
Antonina..............	46,481	30,809
Parahyba..............	1,569,867	1,448,988
Ceará.................	570,543	645,976
Santa Catharina.........	63,836	60,175
Alagoas...............	1,060,601	1,124,394
Sergipe................	357,581	464,588
Espirito Santo..........	....	....
Rio Grande do Norte....	187,451	211,053
Piauhy................	36,526	65,113
Mato Grosso...........	23,864	118,750
TOTAL.........	$48,123,731	$53,421,590

FOREIGN COUNTRIES.

1859–'60.	1860–'61.	1861–'62.	1862–'63.
$28,796,319	$39,541,898	$28,922,506	$26,405,353
5,411,472	4,211,493	8,395,550	9,014,683
5,552,909	3,722,267	6,169,929	6,235,892
1,255,606	1,024,742	1,378,956	2,361,001
2,956,430	2,670,652	2,302,406	2,786,884
2,440,436	2,447,245	2,171,338	2,016,585
1,205,034	1,097,605	1,235,998	917,199
47,262	105,103	145,887	102,619
207,749	141,488	208,626	84,398
3,816,805	3,243,013	4,279,684	4,206,486
833,190	562,017	2,428,343	536,944
31,903	39,474	59,226	92,392
1,677,651	1,015,380	1,484,870	1,948,967
678,286	621,492	1,016,062	1,141,968
101,207	71,187	41,519	53,684
803,032	658,984	1,505,727	2,382,730
239,749	111,003	394,344	553,190
....	....	....	26,264
339,056	164,037	97,604	236,304
65,719	99,447	100,919	111,556
18,172	31,056	25,811	24,893
$56,478,986	$61,585,581	$60,359,976	$61,239,998

IMPERIAL EXPORTS *to*

ARTICLES EXPORTED.	1857–'58.	1858–'59.
Spirits	$659,181	$460,721
Cotton	3,327,660	2,812,048
Sugar (white)	4,196,980	3,952,541
Sugar (brown)	7,155,925	9,880,890
Hair	170,563	206,966
Cocoa	827,908	660,059
Coffee	21,751,426	25,069,126
Hides (salt)	2,092,794	1,978,717
Hides (dry)	1,462,687	1,622,021
Diamonds	1,154,250	1,524,987
Tobacco	1,187,153	1,523,318
Gum Elastic	621,680	942,261
Rose Wood	263,524	307,497
Slate	1,152,033	874,667
Gold (in dust and bar)	351,791	420,232
Other articles	1,748,174	1,185,551
TOTAL	$48,123,731	$53,421,590

Foreign Countries—continued.

1859–'60.	1860–'61.	1861–'62.	1862–'63.
$285,243	$330,272	$429,185	$409,615
3,216,286	2,341,070	3,893,076	8,408,904
2,024,504	5,527,839	3,699,815	3,503,200
5,836,125		7,968,084	6,137,313
182,298	188,148	172,506	159,466
728,138	840,539	721,029	789,468
30,119,218	39,831,776	29,373,496	28,287,467
3,326,935	4,545,167	2,926,376	2,417,922
1,671,061		1,416,885	1,207,922
1,566,000	1,886,150	2,120,624	2,058,087
2,011,227	1,191,283	2,439,309	3,101,005
1,709,519	1,455,266	1,219,179	1,637,956
482,216	326,845	463,918	391,028
1,057,521	836,572	702,188	757,390
701,016	814,645	1,060,699	388,810
1,061,672	1,470,007	1,753,699	1,585,065
$112,957,972	$123,171,163	$60,359,971	$61,239,998

TABLE *of Chief Articles of Importation.*

ARTICLES.	1st Period, 1852–'53 and 1856–'57.	2d Period. 1857–'58 and 1861–'62.	1862–'63.
	Average Value.	Average Value.	
Oils	$307,811	$502,576	$463,366
Fish	1,169,907	1,662,224	744,766
Spirits	369,568	810,218	728,736
Shoes and boots	389,458	753,635	617,558
Meat	760,022	2,414,685	2,748,734
Coal	678,930	1,220,241	1,038,171
Leather	441,325	430,857	487,533
Drugs	501,619	761,204	499,805
Wheat flour	2,304,071	4,259,818	2,461,313
Iron goods	1,986,327	3,094,006	2,603,943
Iron	314,501	651,849	725,364
Earthenware and glass	878,676	909,181	940,875
Machinery	113,095	360,956	425,464
Butter	750,977	1,043,588	1,103,163
Manufactures—			
Cotton	4,593,188	1,641,609	11,913,703
Wool	2,720,358	2,914,139	1,983,529
Linen	1,289,332	1,388,140	1,085,199
Silk	1,218,240	1,587,824	1,093,859
Mixed	2,011,492	1,406,686	1,243,031
Gold and silver money	3,690,043	2,390,202	4,194,444
Gold and silver work	1,155,024	2,005,744	1,149,371
Powder	216,965	272,217	300,797
Salt	387,578	513,054	584,038
Wines	1,653.429	2,141,969	2,354,369

TABLE *of Chief Articles of Exportation.*

ARTICLES.	1st Period. 1852–'53 and 1856–'57. Average Value.	2d Period. 1857–'58 and 1861–'62. Average Value.	1862–'63.
Spirits	$471,944	$432,921	$409,616
Cotton	2,730,836	3,118,028	8,408,904
Sugar	9,602,268	10,048,541	9,640,514
Hair	207,823	184,095	159,466
Cocoa	379,236	755,535	789,468
Coffee	21,995,310	29,229,018	28,287,467
Hides (salt)	1,596,253	4,208,529	2,417,294
Hides (dry)	1,632,093		1,207,423
Diamonds	1,825,454	1,650,401	2,058,088
Tobacco	1,081,171	1,670,458	3,101,005
Gum Elastic	1,168,498	1,189,561	1,637,956
Maté	668,104	924,596	757,391
Gold in dust or bar	90,934	669,676	388,812

QUANTITIES OF ARTICLES EXPORTED.

Articles	Unit	1st Period	2d Period	1862–'63
Spirits	gal.	2,875,340	2,189,807	2,995,186
Cotton	lbs.	31,233,184	24,423,904	34,740,096
Sugar	"	270,411,968	260,587,360	323,895,008
Hair	"	1,526,080	1,299,648	1,202,144
Cocoa	"	73,238,184	8,332,736	10,020,864
Coffee	"	360,496,928	356,245,728	279,172,544
Hides (salt)	"	502,796	594,152	675,562
Hides (dry)	"	13,235,520	11,379,296	12,294,656
Diamonds	oz.	1,523	1,213	1,556
Tobacco	lbs.	18,258,176	16,817,088	36,494,944
Gum Elastic	"	4,578,080	4,626,472	6,672,416
Maté	"	13,982,272	16,614,176	19,365,728
Gold in dust or bar	oz.	6,299	46,234	24,799

IMPERIAL IMPORTS *from Foreign Countries,*

FROM	TOTAL, 1853–'54.	TOTAL, 1862–'63.
British Possessions......	$23,249,739	$25,382,849
Hanse Towns...........	2,596,156	268,966
Belgium................	892,978	504,055
Portuguese Possessions...	2,856,374	2,983,068
Sardinian States.........	328,562	293,786
River Plate............	2,237,023	3,275,288
Imperial Ports..........	344,108	453,701
Spain.................	363,257	927,275
Denmark...............	131,067	34,055
Sweden................	122,549	58,337
French Possessions......	4,977,549	9,191,287
Austria................	337,396	396,864
United States..........	4,026,741	352,206
Holland...............	30,041	65,601
Fishery................		1,078
African Ports not specified	415,887	146,183
Other Ports not specified.		112,097
TOTAL.........	$42,919,376	$49,536,356

showing the Import at each Port in 1862–'63.

RIO DE JANEIRO.	BAHIA.	PERNAMBUCO.
$12,835,086	$4,307,216	$4,155,188
827,386	582,548	293,181
236,183	58,505	52,627
1,097,581	615,479	438,002
184,286	63,982	18,657
1,982,071	640,508	304,339
36,490	268,457	49.639
370,819	144,223	114,871
12,392	2,317	....
43,193	6,275	1,444,388
538,584	1,448,192	76,328
195,357	95,359	567,298
1,089,056	137,988	20,016
....	45,589	....
....	....	....
....	146,183	....
....	....	....
$24,810,802	$8,568,771	$7,534,539

IMPERIAL IMPORTS *from Foreign Countries, showing*

FROM	MARANHAO.	PARA.
British Possessions......	$1,053,323	$1,075,794
Hanse Towns	14,902	74,093
Belgium................	15,386	24,811
Portuguese Possessions...	179,069	367,428
Sardinian States.........	....	....
River Plate	....	....
Imperial Ports	4,179	2,557
Spain	26,941	22,877
Denmark	....	4,824
Sweden	....	....
French Possessions......	361,279	225,561
Austria	8,592	5,517
United States...........	138,576	431,591
Holland	....	....
Fishery	....	....
African Ports not specified	....	....
Other Ports not specified..	....	....
TOTAL..........	$1,802,201	$2,235,153

the Import at each Port in 1862–'63—continued.

Rio Grande do Sul.	Porto Alegre.	Uruguayana.	Santos.
$507,301	$20,492	....	731,546
364,463	293,643	....	120,012
97,377	12,943	....	3,566
191,724	13,399	....	75,747
11,941	9,394	....	5,521
10,643	6,647	$67,554	502
15,301	5,416	....	28,056
222,281	....	....	14,214
....	....	....	....
....	....	....	....
233,515	....	....	24,049
12,138	....	....	....
151,073	....	....	6,534
....	....	....	....
....	....	....	....
....	....	....	....
....	....	....	....
$1,862,761	$361,934	$67,554	$1,009,767

IMPERIAL IMPORTS *from Foreign Countries, showing*

FROM	PARANAGUA.	ANTONINA.
British Possessions	....	....
Hanse Towns...........	....	....
Belgium...............	....	....
River Plate	$135,801	$504
Imperial Ports..........	15,838	....
Spain	....	....
Denmark	....	....
French Possessions	....	....
Austria................	....	....
Fishery................	....	....
Other Ports not specified.	20	....
TOTAL.........	$151,689	$504

FROM	ALAGOAS.	SERGIPE.
British Possessions	$44,162	$12,209
Portuguese Possessions...	264	4,098
Imperial Ports..........	7,242	4,376
Spain	....	215
Denmark...............	....	5,621
Sweden................	....	3,369
French Possessions......	202	....
Other Ports not specified.	....	....
TOTAL.........	$51,870	$29,888

the Import at each Port in 1862–'63—continued.

Parahiba.	Ceara.	Santa Catharina.
$24,576	$500,742	$7,077
....	60,956	53,478
....	....	3,174
....	....	76,197
837	6,857	4,819
5,740	....	....
....	8,849	....
....	67,486	....
....	2,672	....
....	....	1,078
....	....	....
$31,143	$647,562	$145,824

Espirito Santo.	Rio Grande do Norte.	Piauhy.	Mato Grosso.
....	....	$106,627	....
....	$221	....	....
$1,976	1,641	15	....
....	....	....	....
....	....	....	....
....	....	....	....
....	....	218	....
....	....	....	$111,896
$1,476	$1,862	$106,860	$111,896

IMPORTS FROM

—	1857–'58.	1858–'59.	1859–'60.
Rio de Janeiro....	$34,769,873	$34,270,176	$30,114,706
Bahia...........	9,839,765	9,732,220	8,102,970
Pernambuco......	12,392,020	11,643,289	9,746,055
Maranhao........	1,815,500	1,974,506	1,570,626
Para............	1,844,302	1,873,182	2,354,948
Rio Grande do Sul.	2,105,015	2,265,444	2,603,099
Port Alegre......	360,801	281,232	343,981
Uruguayana......	424,551	180,978	230,361
Santos..........	204,297	187,081	283,766
Paranagua.......	75,691	110,666	37,471
Antonina........	2,826	2,565	561
Parahyba........	145,191	123,456	70,124
Ceara...........	551,507	458,993	453,030
Santa Catharina...	54,515	81,834	87,481
Alagoas.........	188,461	247,014	79,245
Sergipe.........	40,454	27,681	13,589
Espirito Santo.....	530	496	234
Rio Grande do Norte.........	248,058	160,912	255,849
Piauhy..........	69,530	85,249	91,449
Mato Grosso......	37,800	54,185	88,875
TOTAL......	$65,220,087	$43,861,309	$56,513,997

FOREIGN COUNTRIES.

1860–'61.	1861–'62.	Average.	1862–'63.
$36,489,915	$49,111,417	$37,951,217	$24,860,802
7,053,774	8,692,500	3,484,247	8,568,721
8,713,029	8,919,160	10,287,711	7,534,539
1,445,901	1,631,735	1,687,663	1,802,201
4,352,372	1,809,696	2,144,900	2,235,657
2,834,317	2,570,032	2,475,581	1,862,761
470,191	550,321	401,305	361,917
148,923	103,809	227,714	68,550
687,415	888,602	450,242	1,009,402
28,791	39,742	56,353	151,842
....	2,267	1,644	504
113,489	18,503	94,192	36,184
444,682	508,337	493,310	649,064
145,943	106,620	95,378	145,824
38,549	38,650	118,384	51,876
7,804	23,806	22,666	29,890
235	994	498	1,976
104,944	14,187	166,790	1,863
127,633	128,513	100,365	106,360
102,778	104,701	77,068	111,896
$61,860,171	$55,265,599	$60,044,230	$49,536,856

IMPORTS FROM

—	1857–'58.	1858–'59.	1859–'60.
Oils	$466,493	$543,874	$522,962
Fish	2,121,091	2,265,272	1,804,510
Spirits	625,898	650,508	595,300
Boots & Shoes	787,242	792,936	788,231
Meat	1,567,333	2,051,669	1,709,642
Coal	787,205	1,053,713	1,060,353
Hats	1,000,129	853,008	883,437
Leather	496,820	438,087	451,417
Drugs	614,801	721,571	1,054,740
Wheat flour	4,535,639	4,352,867	5,342,931
Iron goods	2,653,982	3,327,915	2,827,003
Iron	752,683	741,214	570,862
Earthenware and glass	1,189,490	946,225	792,974
Machinery	240,182	366,729	449,344
Butter	946,446	1,161,925	1,179,994
Manufactures:			
Cotton	17,739,842	1,895,948	13,757,489
Wool	4,132,117	3,029,757	2,891,785
Linen	1,484,065	1,430,898	1,493,109
Silk	1,869,284	1,803,277	1,702,766
Mixed	1,599,574	1,662,339	1,265,816
Coin	3,340,256	2,924,424	2,022,592
Gold and silver work	2,458,960	2,997,626	1,061,766
Paper	5,575,850	440,775	514,529
Powder	271,738	253,127	280,072
Clothing	728,547	721,272	817,659
Salt	583,251	446,650	564,397
Wines	1,547,403	1,945,644	2,855,181
Other articles	10,058,820	9,083,193	6,733,184
TOTAL	$65,220,086	$63,861,309	$56,513,997

Foreign Countries—completed.

1860–'61.	1861–'62.	Average.	1862–'63.
$496,108	$482,943	$502,576	$464,866
1,362,817	757,428	1,662,209	744,766
704,216	1,475,172	810,218	728,736
739,618	660,154	753,635	617,558
2,784,309	4,005,472	2,414,685	2,748,734
1,297,191	1,402,732	1,220,091	1,038,171
718,890	686,546	828,402	696,510
383,427	384,507	430,856	487,533
745,213	619,603	761,204	499,805
3,642,807	2,899,893	4,254,818	1,461,314
3,561,943	3,099,185	3,094,006	2,603,943
678,457	516,006	651,840	725,364
809,723	812,477	909,150	920,870
346,421	382,105	365,956	420,463
1,003,998	925,579	1,043,588	1,103,163
17,217,763	17,464,384	16,416,086	11,913,703
2,558,337	1,958,492	2,914,139	1,983,024
1,349,594	1,183,037	1,088,140	1,085,195
1,494,024	1,069,771	1,587,824	1,093,859
1,106,909	1,398,790	1,406,686	1,243,036
2,661,034	1,012,503	2,390,204	2,194,443
1,607,868	902,651	1,005,599	1,149,370
603,134	544,579	535,774	496,748
271,669	284,031	272,067	300,798
804,494	632,963	741,727	865,448
406,335	564,636	513,054	584,038
2,778,757	2,082,865	2,141,949	2,354,369
9,224,414	7,061,574	8,532,238	8,005,019
$61,860,173	$55,165,095	$60,544,230	$49,536,356

www.ingramcontent.com/pod-product-compliance
Lightning Source LLC
LaVergne TN
LVHW020246110826
845151LV00003B/1033

* 9 7 8 1 4 2 5 5 2 9 1 2 3 *